Supply Chain Planning for the Process Industry

Supply Chain Consultants, Inc

5460 Fairmont Drive, Wilmington DE 19808

Phone (302) 738-9215 • Fax (302) 454-7680

CONTRIBUTORS

Ken Fordyce, Jeff Howard, Don Shobrys, and all the consultants
that worked in the front lines of supply chain planning
implementations, often with no recognition and little gratitude.

LIBRARY OF CONGRESS CATALOGING-IN-PUBLICATION DATA

Supply Chain Consultants -

Supply Chain Planning in the Process Industry

ISBN-10: 0-92823148-1-7

ISBN-13: 978-0-9823148-1-4

Contents

Planning the Process Supply Chain

According to Wikipedia, process manufacturing is the branch of manufacturing that is associated with formulas and manufacturing recipes, and can be contrasted with discrete manufacturing, which is concerned with bills of material and routing. This may suffice at a high level, but there are other distinct process manufacturing characteristics that influence how planning is done. These differences do not generally have an impact on a company's organization or how it manages its finances. For this reason, ERP systems translate from a discrete application to a process application fairly well at the "corporate" level.

As you get closer to actual manufacturing, though, the differences can create real issues for supply chain planning. The unique characteristics of the process industry require specialized solutions that can cope with managing material delivery and capacity utilization simultaneously.

We'll illustrate some of these characteristics through examples from chemicals, food, and semiconductors because together they represent a significant portion of the process industry.

Key Planning Characteristics

Inverted Bill of Material

In a discrete environment, many parts are used to make subassemblies which in turn are put together to make the final product. In other words, many small parts come together to make a product. For example, it takes fifty thousand or more parts to create an automobile.

Process manufacturing is the reverse. A few products or ingredients result in thousands of different products. In plastic manufacturing, ethylene may result in many different products depending on how it is processed. In semiconductors, a single wafer may result in many different final parts and in food manufacturing, a single ingredient like oranges could result in many products like fresh juice, oranges, dried oranges, frozen juice in different packages, and so on.

Importance of Capacity

In the process supply chains, the high investment and high technology operations are usually done early in the production process. A key element of the production process at Sunsweet is the process used to remove the pit from the plum. The pineapple processer Dole has specialized machines to peel and core the fruit prior to processing. Chemical manufacturers often have extruders or autoclaves to polymerize the resin prior to packaging. In semiconductors, the Fab facility that does the initial processing is the single most costly step.

Because the assets that perform the processing at the start of the manufacturing process are expensive, their capacity utilization is important and often significantly affects the final product cost. In a discrete environment, the primary manufacturing issue is to make sure that the right part is available for the next production step. In process manufacturing, managing the capacity of the high value assets is as important as ensuring the timely flow of product.;

NG THE PROCESS SUPPLY CHAIN

us Products

onment, a product is either good or bad. Each part has
and if the part meets these, then it is acceptable. In the
more complicated. When a lot is manufactured, it has its
ristics. In the chemical industry this might be melt index
ent. In semiconductors, it might be the speed which the
chip will tolerate. Typically, the process can be controlled so that these
characteristics fall within a range. However, even in this range, the lot might
be acceptable for some customers, but not for others.

Creating a separate product name for each customer is not a reliable solution,
because the acceptable range for a customer can and does change over
time. For supply chain planning, this can become complicated because the
inventory of a product is not homogenous. It may be the case that there is
plenty of inventory available but no inventory that will meet a particular
customer's requirements.

Raw material Variability

The process manufacturer may also encounter non-homogeneity in the raw
materials. Many times, each lot of the delivered product needs to be tested so
that the manufacturing process can be tuned to the input material. For
example, a refinery that is running crude with one sulphur content cannot use
the exact same settings if the crude has significantly higher or lower sulphur
content.

Very often, critical raw materials in the process industry are generally
commodities which are traded. Often the price and availability determines
what the manufacturer has to cope with. For example, a typical refinery
deals with 15 or 20 crudes in a month. The crude mix could change every
two weeks and each change requires resetting the parameters for running
the crudes through.

Finished products on the other hand, are required to have reproducible
characteristics. For example, it would not do to have large chunks of
pineapple in a 12 oz can one month and smaller chunks the next month
even though the size of the fruit purchased varies.

For this reason, the manufacturing process has to be tuned continuously
to cope with variable raw material inputs.

Complex Industry-Dependent Issues

Industry-dependent issues range from high investment and inflexible facilities in chemicals to variable and time varying yields in semiconductors. In many cases, product changes cost time and money. But this is not the only challenge. Product changes can also have variability associated with them. In chemicals, the same product transition could vary significantly because of operator experience or even the weather.

Facilities at the beginning of the production process tend to be capital intensive. In semiconductors, the Fab facility can run into the hundreds of millions. In chemicals, the bulk of the capital is used to build the facilities that create the products for other processes like blending and packaging.

Because of the need to utilize these assets efficiently at the beginning of the production process, there is a desire to produce large quantities of one product before switching to another product. On the other hand, the market would like the responsiveness associated with small production runs. There is constant tension between making short runs (to speed up delivery and minimize inventory) and the need to utilize capacity effectively.

Other issues include seasonal demand, uncertain crop yields, stringent requirements in food manufacturing, and regulatory control in chemicals. Food manufacturing companies have unique challenges because they often have to plan for demand within available supply. For example, food cooperatives are sometimes limited by the seasonal crop yield; meat packers must forecast demand that adds up to whole animals. (It does not make any sense to forecast demand that requires cattle with 1 tail and two heads)

Most commercially available planning systems cannot account for capacity and material restrictions simultaneously. In addition, as retailers consolidate, there is increasing pressure on manufacturers to reduce margins, and also to provide products that require less preparation at the wholesale/retail end. This creates additional processing and cost for the manufacturer.

In semiconductors, products are constantly introduced. Profits and earnings are intimately tied to how quickly a product can be brought to market. Often a 3 to 4 month delay will result in a 30 percent reduction in total revenue for the product because of price erosion.

Another unique characteristic is that the manufacturing process in the Fab is highly variable. Typically, yields improve significantly over time, while prices decline.

It is also not unusual for manufacturing steps in semiconductors to be spread out over different countries. Production needs to be coordinated between these outlying facilities. This is especially challenging because the downstream processes are often sub-contracted.

Improving Supply Chain Planning

Most currently available commercial tools are geared towards discrete industry application. Optimization within process industries often requires sophisticated tools which require training and support. Many vendors are simply not equipped to address these issues.

Unfortunately, many businesses still regard supply chain planning as a function that is independent of their manufacturing characteristics. Vendors and consultants encourage this view because it allows them to expand their market. Another popular view that is encouraged by software vendors is that chain planning is a software system issue – one that can be bought by implementing better systems.

Our experience is that world-class supply chains are not a one-time systems event. To remain competitive, a business needs to maintain the health of the supply chain planning processes across four key dimensions.

Functionality

The basic building block of any good supply chain is Functional Excellence. Each of the supply chain functions, plan, source, make, and deliver, should be created using competitive business practices and supported with the appropriate technology. For the process industry, this means that any quantitative model must address the issues of capacity and material requirements simultaneously. Any discrete solution that focuses only on the coordination of materials (like MRP) will cause duplicate and redundant practices to creep into the workflow.

Functional excellence is relatively easy to address because the effort required is focused on a small identifiable area.

Adaptability

Change is a constant because every business environment evolves. To stay relevant, the supply chain must evolve as well. In other words, the systems and practices have to change to keep pace with changes in technology, business climate, and markets.

Take the case of a food cooperative like Sunsweet. Crop yields vary from year to year. Manufacturing has to balance the available supply with consumer demand constantly. It does not have the luxury of exploring additional sources of supply like non-cooperatives. The supply chain has to adapt and optimize through the varying periods of short supply and over supply.

Process manufacturers are generally at the start of the consumer supply chain. Products that they manufacture are processed by other companies and distributers before being delivered to the end customer. Demand is placed on the process manufacturer through orders which tend to be aggregated due to lot size considerations and inventory policies. For example, a manufacturer of plastic consumer products may run his line constantly but order the resin periodically in railcar or truckload quantities. As a result, the resin manufacturer sees sporadic demand in truckload quantities.

The aggregation of demand gets magnified when the customer sees fluctuation in his demand and tries to react to it using simple inventory rules. The typical process manufacturer has to deal with this magnified demand variability and the supply chain has to manage through these cycles of "boom and bust."

Integration

For a supply chain to function well, the individual elements need to operate in a coordinated manner. Functional integration has many facets. First, the data needs to be consistent. This is often done through an ERP implementation. Supply chain planning is highly data intensive. While it is not necessary to have perfect data, it is necessary to have reliable data at people's fingertips.

Second, the metrics across different functions should be in harmony. Such harmony is best achieved by creating business metrics that are cross functional. For example, a measurement of schedule changes due to inaccurate forecasts may be more relevant than a measurement of forecast accuracy alone. The metrics that measure the efficiency of a function should not conflict with overall business goals.

Third, the software and data should be available on demand. This usually means that the relevant data and tools must be made available to planners on their desktop. Supply chain planning deals with uncertainty and must support users in making decisions quickly and consistently in an uncertain environment.

Fourth, integration across business functions is critical for operational efficiency. When a business function is outsourced, the integration dimension becomes much more important. In semiconductors, some of the less value-adding manufacturing steps are outsourced. In other companies, the transportation function may be outsourced. When a function is outsourced, steps must be taken to provide visibility into the outsourced function because lack of visibility often increases uncertainty, which, in turn, causes people to build buffers to protect themselves.

Leverage

The leverage dimension is probably the least understood because it deals with exploiting synergies across different businesses. For businesses within a common financial entity, leverage can be achieved in the following ways:

- Adopting common work practices and common data systems.

- Allocating resources to maximize overall margins.

- Exploiting economies of scale where appropriate, e.g., software licenses and training.

In chemicals, it can mean leveraging across different supply chains that consume a common ingredient. For example, in a chemical supply chain, propylene and ethylene ratios can be proactively set to exploit market demand and to maximize margins.

Frequently, to leverage successfully, a business has to look for synergies outside its immediate supply chain. For example, if the product is dense like bleach, transport efficiencies can be gained by combining its distribution with a bulky product like cereal, to mitigate the effect of both weight and volume restrictions.

About this Book

While the basic building blocks of functionality, adaptability, integration, and leverage are applicable to all industries, process industries represent a challenge in how these are used to extract value from the supply chain. Much that has been written about improving supply chain management is not geared towards the professional who works in the process supply chain. Either the literature is at too general a level to be useful, or it is written with the largest audience in mind – the discrete industry. Software has evolved in the same way. Software companies have naturally targeted the largest market which is indeed discrete manufacturing.

Supply chain professionals face a frustrating task when they try to use the principles articulated in the literature and the software available on the market. At a conceptual level, there are many similarities between the discrete and process environment. But agreement at the conceptual level does not necessarily translate to successful implementation. When software systems and practices that do not account for fundamental process characteristics are mandated, it eventually leads to the development of parallel systems because the folks on the ground have to deal with practicalities. In many companies, the planning tasks and supply chain management continues to be done in an informal way with spreadsheets and desktop tools with the results being fed to the officially mandated supply chain system.

The purpose of this book is to highlight some of the challenges specific to the process industry. This collection of papers is meant for those who hold an operational view of their business. It illustrates some of the key notions that are important for process supply chains and is meant as a resource for those seeking to improve their planning processes and software.

History of Supply Chain Planning in the Process Industry

By Don Shobrys

Companies have benefited from Supply Chain Planning (SCP) techniques for over 30 years. SCP techniques are a collection of well established solution methods made more accessible and effective by incremental improvements in a wide range of technologies. This view may not have too much sizzle, but it means that there is a broad experience base that companies trying to implement SCP can draw on.

There is a wide range of diversity in the perspectives that consultants, vendors, market analysts, and customers have on SCP. This diversity stems from a number of factors.

- Business systems (legacy, MRP II, and ERP) are transaction based. Much of the analysis that occurs in SCP is above the transaction level of detail. The systems architecture of transaction systems limited their planning and scheduling capabilities. SCP is still new to many of the people that have worked with transaction based systems.

- Prior to 1990, much of the work with SCP was done with in-house development. The plethora of vendors and products is a relatively new phenomenon.

- Many major consulting firms did not become active in this area until a well defined group of products and vendors emerged.

- The people currently covering SCP come from a wide range of industries. SCP penetrated different industries at different points in time. The timing was greatly influenced by when companies were able to manage the data needed to describe their business. The process industries saw early use, while use in discrete manufacturing occurred later.

- Vendors, many of whom are using similar solution methods, have differentiated themselves with creative descriptions and enthusiastic claims.

- Contributions to SCP have come from APICS, artificial intelligence, computer science, decision support systems, industrial engineering, logistics, management science, operations research, and production operations management among others. Each area uses its own vocabulary. In addition to creating confusion (even "planning" and "scheduling" do not have standard meanings), this also creates opportunities to reinvent the wheel.

SCP evolved from continuous improvement coupled with the synergistic incorporation of new technologies. Let us step through this evolution. This narrative is not totally comprehensive as it is heavily influenced by my own experiences. One key source of bias is that virtually all of the 100+ companies I have worked with have significant complexity and cost in their manufacturing operations. The projects either focused on manufacturing, or took an integrated view across procurement, manufacturing, and distribution.

SCP BC (Before Computers)

Some key concepts embodied in SCP predate the existence of computers. One is the Gantt chart, which lets people view schedules and interactively update them. This concept came into being around the turn of the 20th century, and since then people have created and maintained Gantt charts with colored rubber bands, blocks, pegs, and 3" by 5" cards. The notion of using mathematical models to solve planning problems occurred at least as early as the 1940's, when both the US and Soviet Union had people manually applying a new optimization technique called linear programming to solve logistics problems related to the war effort.

The 1950's and Early 1960's – Computers Become Available

In the late 1950's and early 1960's, large companies started leasing computer time and then acquiring computers. Computers were used to look at a portion of planning problems, like optimizing around a few key material or energy balances subject to product demand and capacity constraints, or finding the lowest cost recipe for a batch of product. Linear programming was commonly used, and the models were the equivalent of small spreadsheet applications (40 to 60 balance equations and 60 to 100 decision variables). Two of the first companies to provide optimization based planning tools were founded during this period (Bonner and Moore in 1957 and Haverly Systems in 1962).

A definition of optimization may help avoid confusion. A strict definition of an optimization technique is a solution method that is guaranteed to find the "best" answer to a problem, and is smart enough to know when it finds it. In addition, it gives a good idea of how long it will take to solve.

In today's common usage "optimization" is often applied to solution methods that simply look for improvement, and are not guaranteed to find the best solution. The techniques that simply look for improvement are also called heuristics, and they are often used with time limits or tolerances ("Give me the best solution you can find in ten minutes"). Confusion occurs when these definitions of optimization are used interchangeably, which sometimes occurs within a single sales presentation. Linear programming meets the strict definition of optimization, recognizes constraints, and often uses the economics around a problem (costs and revenues) to define the "best" solution.

Mid 1960's through Early 1970's – Applications Evolve

As computers continued to evolve, people were able to take a more complete view of planning problems. Tools evolved that considered an entire manufacturing site and identified the slate of operations that minimized cost or maximized profit. Some companies connected the computers and programs that optimized product recipes to the production equipment. People also started looking at distribution problems, while companies like Exxon built tools that gave an integrated view across feedstock acquisition, manufacturing, and distribution.

The size of production applications went from hundreds of decision variables in the early 1960's to thousands of decision variables around 1970, to tens of thousands in the late 1970's. Solution techniques like linear programming were also extended to address more difficult problems, like the yes/no decisions associated with adding production capacity, selecting production technology, or picking sites for distribution centers.

These applications often occurred in the process industries and at a planning level. Large refining and chemical companies like Amoco, Chevron, Exxon, Marathon, and Shell were aggressive about purchasing large computers and placing them at manufacturing sites. These companies were also aggressive about data capture and integration. The business motivation was there because optimization techniques fit well with many of their manufacturing processes, and with the characteristics of their distribution networks.

Many companies developed their own tools internally for mainframe computing environments. The programs that solve linear programming problems were available from a number of sources. A classic example was MPS (later MPSX) from IBM. Some companies used existing solvers while others wrote their own. Many companies wrote code around solvers to manage the problems they would address. This custom code would collect data, organize it in the form needed by the optimizers, control the solution process, and then generate reports. Assembler, Cobol, FORTRAN, and PL/1 were all used as development languages. These programs ran in batch mode, and user interfaces were initially line editors and then full screen editors. Exxon even published a book about their planning system (2).

Computer based tools were developed to address elements of scheduling problems. Simulation was being used for design of manufacturing and distribution facilities. Simulation tools were also developed to calculate the consequences of schedules in terms of capacity and material consumption. Logic was developed for specific scheduling issues like sequencing activities or calculating lot sizes. Much of this was developed in-house using user interfaces and modes of interaction similar to those for planning.

Simulation based scheduling tools started to emerge in the 1970's. Pritsker was one early source. Another early product was CPPS from IBM, which started as a batch product and was converted to interactive use around 1975.

The major refining companies were active users of planning tools in the 1970s. Other industries were also actively using planning and scheduling applications. A series of internally developed tools had an integral role in the evolution of Federal Express (3). By the early 1980's Kelly Springfield, a tire manufacturer, and Philip Morris had planning and scheduling applications in place. Paper companies like St Regis and International Paper were also either implementing tools or had applications in place.

The 1980's – The Business Press Discovers SCP

Creative Output Inc., a company led by Eli Goldratt, was featured in the September 5, 1983 issue of Fortune Magazine. Their product, OPT, applied a series of de-bottlenecking algorithms in a batch processing mode. A very aggressive sales organization capable of generating million dollar deals had captured a number of customers in discrete manufacturing. Creative Output withdrew from the market shortly after a legal dispute with M&M/Mars over expected benefits (4). Eli Goldratt expanded his Theory of Constraints philosophy and went on to a career as a well published manufacturing guru, while Creative Output alumni became active in the SCP arena with i2. The same Fortune article briefly mentioned Numetrix Decision Science, which later split into Numetrix and Chesapeake Decision Sciences, two early SCP suppliers with interactive products that provided memory resident analysis.

During this time, articles on the use of SCP solution methods and products started appearing in Business Week, the Chicago Tribune, the New York Times, the Wall Street Journal, and the Washington Post. The biggest flurry of media attention centered on an algorithm developed by a young AT&T researcher named Narendra Karmarkar in 1984. This new technique for solving linear programming problems got front page treatment, and was aggressively promoted by AT&T as "a real breakthrough" that was "designed to solve ...previously unsolvable problems." AT&T bundled the algorithm with one of their computers, priced it at $8.9 million, and called the product Korbx (5,6).

Rumor has it that only one sale of Korbx occurred, but virtually all modern LP solvers have incorporated solution methods based on Karmarkar's algorithm.

The 1980's also saw the introduction of personal computers and spreadsheets. Spreadsheets were a two edged sword. On the positive side, they introduced people to the use of interactive analysis for forecasting, planning and scheduling. In a number of companies with existing mainframe applications, users built simple approximations of the existing tools and migrated to them. Unfortunately, when mainframe applications died, so did the infrastructure that was collecting and validating the underlying data. Many of the refining companies that aggressively developed planning systems during the 1970's went backwards with respect to data quality and tool accuracy in the late 1980's.

In the mid 1980's, many major chemical companies realized that they were reaching limits in their ability to offset decreasing margins with improvements to their manufacturing processes, so they started examining their supply chain activities. BASF, DOW, DuPont, and Rohm and Haas all started initiatives with planning and scheduling tools. They used products, tools they developed in house, or products that they modified internally. The intent was to have a true supply chain focus, rather than implement point solutions for functional silos like manufacturing or distribution.

The MRP II vendors like Marcam and Datalogix responded by marketing their capabilities to the process industries. Some companies delayed development of SCP tools while they determined whether their planning and scheduling needs would be met with MRP and CRP. By the early 1990's many major chemical companies had selected an SCP vendor.

Many major airlines also had implemented sophisticated planning and scheduling systems. The AADT group of American Airlines (now Sabre Technologies) started building those systems for other airlines.

The late 1980's also saw the emergence of artificial intelligence (AI) and expert systems. Companies were formed to apply AI to production planning and scheduling, and investors and clients expected that once intractable problems would become tractable. DuPont and IBM were aggressive in combining AI with existing technologies and generating applications. IBM developed a dispatch scheduling system (7). DuPont cosponsored the addition of expert system capabilities to the optimization, simulation, and heuristics in the MIMI product from Chesapeake Decision Sciences, Inc. The expert system was used in conjunction with those other capabilities for data validation, incorporation of heuristics, solution interpretation, and making planning output useful for scheduling (8). Real time expert systems products like G2 also emerged at this time. The AI community made subsequent contributions with techniques like constraint based programming and genetic algorithms.

Expectations for AI had been set at an extremely high level. There was disappointment over what AI ultimately delivered, and unfortunately some people still view it as a failure. Many AI developers felt that their technology should only be applied in a pure fashion, so a lot of time and effort went into recreating functionality developed with other tools in the 1960's and 1970's.

The late 1980's also brought graphical user interfaces. Vendors had tried combining a Personal Computer and its native graphics capability with an additional card containing a second processor for more computational horsepower. With the emergence of OSF MOTIF as a graphics standard, interactive graphical user interfaces became a standard part of forecasting, planning, and scheduling tools. This technical innovation had the greatest impact on the marketability of SCP.

There was also a flurry of tools with animation capabilities that sparked an interest in the use of animation for scheduling. While animation has proved useful for design and dispatching applications, interest in animation for scheduling has not been sustained.

The 1990's – The SCP Market Booms and Products Proliferate

Consumer packaged companies (CPG) started to become more active with SCP in the early 1990's. Although there were some early adopters in this market segment, this industry as a whole was slower in using SCP techniques. This is true of the paper industry as well, despite the sophisticated approaches used for trim problems. A number of companies that were able to use relatively simple tools for manufacturing scheduling discovered they needed more sophistication to cover the number of SKU and location combinations they found in their distribution networks.

Many of these companies also made similar discoveries with respect to their forecasting capabilities. The simple tools used to generate revenue forecasts choked on the number of SKU and location combinations needed to provide the level of detail required for operational decisions.

The early 1990's also saw the introduction of imbedded SQL capabilities, allowing SCP tools to interact more dynamically with relational databases. The availability of increasing amounts of computer horsepower at decreasing costs led to new solution methods, and expanded the size and complexity of the problems that were being addressed. Genetic algorithms became available. They grow multiple solutions at once, combining the best features of existing solutions to create new ones. People started using simulated annealing, which will let a solution get worse in the hopes that this will create pathways to even better solutions. Production tools with millions of decisions variables were developed, although if you create an application of this size, you are probably making your life more painful than it has to be.

The 1990's have seen a proliferation of SCP vendors across a wide range of industries. Companies like i2 and Fastman made inroads with electronic assembly, metals, and discrete manufacturing. I2's most dramatic impact on the SCP space was the introduction of brand oriented marketing and sales strategies to what had previously been a technology driven niche market, and soon they were in a race with Manugistics for revenue growth.

The reaction of the marketplace to i2, Manugistics, and others caught the attention of the large consulting firms. They started allocating resources to products based on market success and client preferences, kicking off a slew of relationships.

SCP presented 2 major challenges to the larger consulting firms. It requires depth of application expertise, but the personnel development policies at many of these firms were focused on producing IT generalists who could manage and bring in major engagements. Annual staff turnover of 25% or more also hindered development of technical depth. In addition, rigid application of standard project methodologies can be a very ineffective way to implement SCP. Domain expertise is still needed to determine how to use the project methodology effectively.

The mid 1990's also saw vendors move user interfaces to a Microsoft Windows environment via client server architecture, or move entire applications to a Windows NT environment. In addition to providing more intuitive user interfaces and reporting capabilities, this moved SCP applications into an environment where low cost computer horsepower was increasing at an amazing rate.

The mid 1990's also saw SCP use on the part of the semiconductor companies. These companies are extremely aggressive in changing production technology, and have products with extremely short life cycles. This makes it challenging to provide the knowledge base required for SCP applications, particularly at the scheduling level. Initial use of SCP techniques paralleled that in the process industry as companies like Harris Semiconductor (9), IBM, Intel (10), and Texas Instruments (11) started by developing internal solutions, with mixed results.

Finally, in the mid 1990's, SCP captured the attention of the ERP vendors. Key attractions were the deal sizes generated in SCP sales, a cost per user far above that received by the ERP vendors, and the rapid growth of the SCP market. This kicked off an initial round of partnerships followed by acquisitions and internal development efforts by the ERP vendors. Some feel that, because of their size, the ERP vendors will ultimately dominate SCP. If size was the driving factor, then IBM and AT&T should be dominating this space right now.

This brings us to the present, where we have the Internet, collaborative planning, the role of the supply chain in product design, and a host of other intriguing topics. I am sure that I have missed other companies that contributed to the development of SCP. My apologies to any pioneers that I have omitted.

This brief narrative does show how collective improvements across a number of areas have culminated in what we know today as SCP. The improvements have reduced the barriers to entry for companies seeking to improve their supply chain management functions. Compute power is much cheaper, data can be moved more readily, software products preclude the need for internal development, and the supply of consulting resources continues to expand. Companies seeking to play in this arena still have to address the major challenges associated with implementation:

- developing the infrastructure to provide integrated data of adequate quality,

- developing the internal skills to use these technologies effectively, and

- instilling the discipline to actively use these tools

References

John Layden, The Evolution of Scheduling Logic, APS, pages 23-25, August, 1998.

Kenneth H. Palmer, N. Kenneth Boudwin, Helen A. Patton, A. John Rowland, Jeremy D. Sammes, and David M. Smith, A Model Management Framework for Mathematical Programming, John Wiley and Sons, 1984.

Richard Mason, James McKenney, Walter Carlson, and Duncan Copeland Absolutely, Positively Operations Research: The Federal Express Story, Interfaces 27: March to April 97.

Follow-Up, Fortune Magazine, March 5, 1984.

Jerry E. Bishop, AT&T Maintains Secrecy on Details In Touting Problem-Solving Inventions, The Wall Street Journal, November 26, 1984.

Roger Lowenstein, AT&T Markets Problem Solver, Based on Math Whiz's Find, For $8.9 Million, The Wall Street Journal, August 15, 1988.

Kenneth Fordyce and Gerald Sullivan, Logistic Management Systems (LMS): Integrating Decision Technologies for Dispatch Scheduling in Semiconductor Manufacturing, Chapter 17 in Intelligent Scheduling edited by Monte Zweben and Mark S. Fox, Morgan Kaufman Publishing, 1994.

Joe Faccenda and Duncan A. Rowan, Expert Systems, Chapter 8 in Planning, Scheduling, and Control Integration in the Process Industries, Edited by C. Edward Bodington, McGraw Hill Incorporated, 1995.

Robert C. Leachman, Robert F. Benson, Chihwei Liu, and Dale J. Raar, IMPReSS: An Automated Production-Planning and Delivery-Quotation System at Harris Corporation – Semiconductor Sector, Interfaces 26:1, January – February 1996.

Karl G. Kempf, Intelligently Scheduling Semiconductor Wafer Fabrication, Chapter 18 in Intelligent Scheduling edited by Monte Zweben and Mark S. Fox, Morgan Kaufman Publishing, 1994.

Hugh E. Fargher and Richard A. Smith, Planning in a Flexible Semiconductor Manufacturing Environment, Chapter 19 in Intelligent Scheduling edited by Monte Zweben and Mark S. Fox, Morgan Kaufman Publishing, 1994.

Knowledge Processing for Supply Chain Planning

By Ed Mahler and Harpal Singh

Unique Chemical Challenges

Change is a constant, and organizations who are attempting to manage the complexities of supply and demand across various global business units often struggle with building a common language and framework for monitoring efforts to improve operations performance.

The chemical supply chain is characterized by one or more of the following:

- High fixed costs.

- Manufacturing assets that are relatively inflexible.

- Product transitions which are expensive and variable.

- A bill of materials structure that decomposes a few raw materials into many finished products.

- Production processes that require blending and large runs to make consistent products.

- Raw material prices that fluctuate continuously.

- Finished products that are not homogenous. Customers may require lots with particular specs.

The business climate is just as challenging. Continued pressure on margins, coupled with regulatory pressures, has forced companies to drive towards higher asset utilization and economies of scale. However, the market continues to shift to more specialty products. It is especially challenging to manage these pressures because the existing assets are often built for throughput and not for flexibility.

In today's economy, capital, technology, and labor are highly mobile. Quality and service can no longer distinguish a company because these are the minimum requirements to be a player in the marketplace. What makes one company more competitive than the next is the quality and consistency of the decisions that it makes. Since no company has an insurmountable lead in capital, technology or labor, the winner is the company that uses its organizational knowledge to make robust and "fact-based" decisions consistently.

Often this requires an infrastructure that provides a solid framework for managing organizational knowledge and information. Most organizations will agree that their competitiveness depends on the decisions made using the collective knowledge and expertise of its people, but few companies measure their knowledge, and even fewer can tell you if it is increasing or decreasing.

Different Kinds of Knowledge for Decision Making

Decision making is how a company processes knowledge and initiates actions based on that knowledge. To understand this, let's look at the different kinds of knowledge that are needed in the typical supply chain.

Basic to all decision making are the facts. We like to call these the "laws of physics." This is the knowledge that is indisputable. It might be data like the amount of inventory, or processing rates, or number of orders, and so on. Much of this knowledge can be found in ERP systems or manuals.

Layered on top of this are the rules commonly used to process the facts. We like to call these the "heuristics." These rules may be mathematical in nature. Examples include a mathematical model that balances supply and demand or policies that set safety stocks.

If this was all the knowledge required to make a decision, then all decisions could be automated. The process would be to assemble the data and apply the appropriate heuristic or rule. Unfortunately, this is not the case. Every situation also has a component of what we call "tertiary" knowledge. Tertiary knowledge is not specific to the decision at hand. It is information that changes over time and provides the context within which decisions are made.

Let's look at an example of someone faced with the decision of setting inventory targets. The basic data consists of the inventory available at each location, the projected demand and measures of uncertainty, the available supply and the flexibility of varying the supply, the costs associated with holding inventory, and other quantitative data needed to calculate the targets.

The heuristics consist of the method for calculating the targets. These may be simple rules like "days of supply" or complex multi-echelon formulas.

Consider now the situation of a company that has significant debt on its balance sheet. (Hexion Specialty Chemicals faced precisely this situation in early 2009.) It is not uncommon for a company to have the opportunity of retiring its debt at a discount if the creditor is in need of cash. In such a situation, the company may elect to reduce its service levels temporarily and drive down its inventory by overriding the heuristics, thereby raising the cash to retire the debt.

The knowledge about the financial opportunity is what we call tertiary information. It has two characteristics. First, it is not directly related to the issue at hand which is to set safety stocks. Second, the knowledge is about a transient situation. It may not occur in precisely the same way when calculating safety stocks some other time.

The reality is that the need to process tertiary information is more the rule than an exception. A classic example is the catalyst bed in a reactor. While there may be rules as to how often the catalyst is changed, these rules are often adjusted in practice depending on the actual circumstances which may have very little to do with the reactor or the catalyst. In a period of high demand, manufacturing might elect to run the reactor longer and delay the catalyst change. Although this results in lower overall productivity, it may be necessary to avoid immediate product shortages. Conversely, manufacturing may elect to accelerate the catalyst change if there is an unplanned outage and the reactor is out of commission anyway.

Processing the Knowledge

As far as data or hard facts are concerned, the requirement is that this knowledge be made available to decision makers when they need to process it. In other words, it needs to be prompt, accessible, and accurate at the point of decision making. What many people ignore, however, is that the data that is used to make decisions also has to be *internally consistent*. For example, if inventory information is made available as of 6 a.m. and shipments are made available as of 12 p.m., then the inventory will not reflect the morning's shipments and the decision maker spends an inordinate amount of time reconciling the data.

The rules that use the data (i.e., the heuristics) are usually contained in software or procedures. Depending on the complexity, these may be in spreadsheets or sophisticated software based on mathematical models. All too often, however, we see companies place a great deal of emphasis on integrating and delivering the data and very little emphasis on how the data is used. While it is true that no software or method will function without good data, it is also true that simplistic heuristics often do not take full advantage of good data because they were originally developed as "rules of thumb." Not only do decision makers need accurate data, they also need the tools to make use of the data properly.

There is no system solution to "tertiary data." This is the portion of knowledge that is so unstructured that only people can process it. Companies have repeatedly tried to codify all possible situations, but this is pointless. By definition, tertiary data is ever-changing and its application requires judgment and evaluation of uncertainty. People need to do this, not computers.

All situations require the different kinds of business knowledge. In general, the longer the time horizon, the greater the role of tertiary knowledge. For example, if the decision is about locating a plant, then the knowledge required may include an estimate of political, social, and demographic conditions in the future as well as the usual knowledge about transport costs, labor costs, supply and demand, legal requirements and so on. Much of this changes over time and not all of it may be relevant at any one time. The knowledge needed to make a decision today may not be exactly the same tomorrow.

Decisions that require a fast resolution have to be made without tertiary knowledge. For example, if there is a fire, then the fire alarm has to be activated. Because there is no time for evaluating tertiary information, automation is required. In such situations, it is normal to adopt conservative rules. All of us have had the smoke alarm go off in the kitchen when it was not really required. This is a prime example of a conservative rule.

In a business situation, conservative rules cost money. For example, if the rule is enforced that the reactor will always be back on-line within six hours, we may need a substantial investment in parts as well as labor. While it is true that we might like the reactor on-line within six hours, we might be willing to waive the rule in an economic downturn or over a long weekend. The information that allows a person to decide when and when not to enforce a rule is the tertiary information.

For tertiary information to be used effectively, we need to define a process for decision making. This process defines the boundaries within which a person can adjust the heuristics, as well as the mechanism to escalate a decision to someone else. Without such a framework, there is no mechanism available to incorporate tertiary information. Without such a framework, a decision maker can either choose to enforce all the heuristics all the time or ignore all the heuristics all the time. This is particularly dangerous if more than one person is required to make a decision because the decisions could be totally inconsistent.

At the core of most decisions is balancing the supply and demand in the supply chain. This requires making predictions about future demand and assumptions about the availability of resources. Most companies try to support the supply/demand balance with a Sales and Operations Planning (S&OP) Process. This is a structured process for gathering data and evaluating options. The S&OP process culminates in a meeting where decisions are made and communicated.

The process that precedes the S&OP meeting is targeted at gathering the facts and applying the heuristics. It is also used to develop options and alternatives based on the available tertiary information. The S&OP meeting itself is usually where a consensus is developed based on the tertiary information that is available.

Making Good Decisions All the Time

All companies make great decisions some of the time. But the key to business success is to make good decisions *all* the time. Company success is much like investment success. It requires a disciplined process to evaluate ever changing data and make rigorous judgments about the future. Not all the decisions will necessarily work out, but the hope is that the large majority of decisions will have a positive outcome.

Decision making in the supply chain is no different. Consistency and the rigorous evaluation of facts are required for sustainable success.

The key elements required to move an organization towards supply chain planning improvements are summarized in the chart below. Basic to any improvements is a framework for consistent decision making. Often companies use the Sales and Operations Planning process as the basis for tactical supply chain planning. Putting the process in place empowers people in the organization because it clearly defines roles and responsibilities. At the same time, the metrics need to change as well from those that are directed at individual departments to those that encourage collaborative behavior.

A process is a prerequisite, but it will not achieve the benefits without delivering the data to the decision makers. Data that participants need is of two kinds: the quantitative data like demand, inventory, costs, and performance, and also the rules that the organization wants to impose to process this quantitative information. To the extent that these rules are codified, they need to reside in a central repository that can be conveniently accessed.

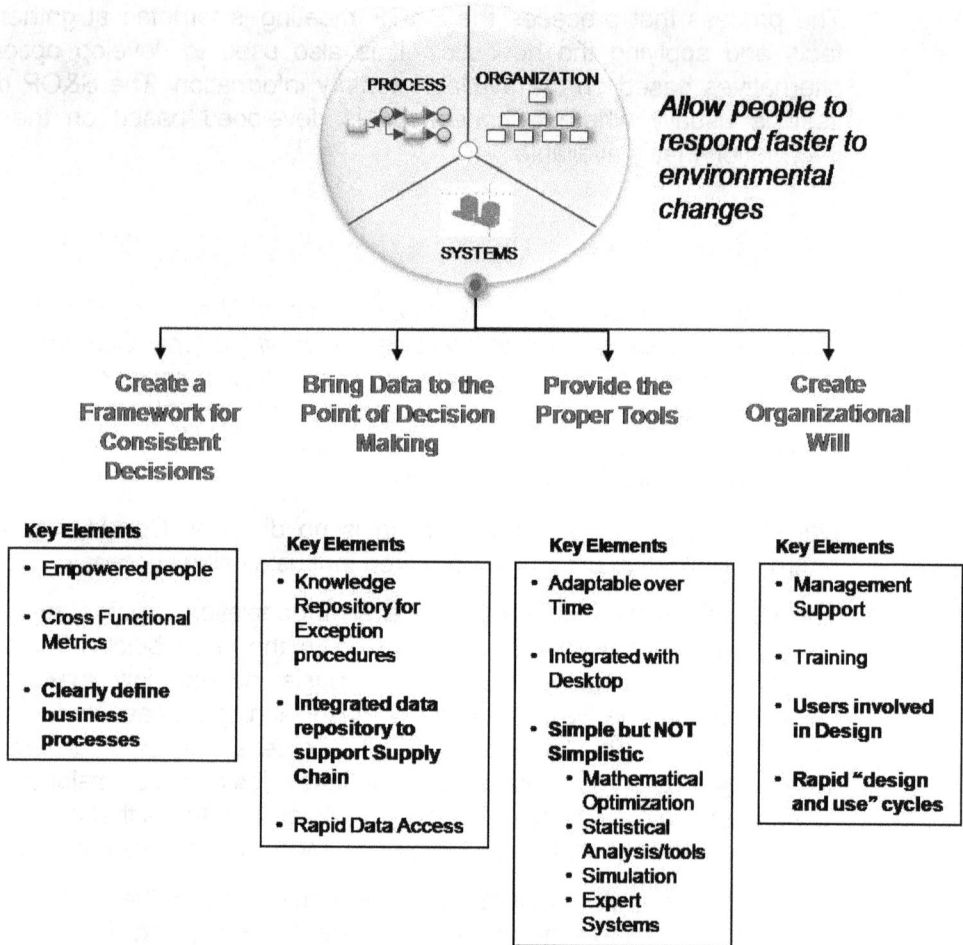

PROCESS **ORGANIZATION**

SYSTEMS

Allow people to respond faster to environmental changes

Create a Framework for Consistent Decisions	Bring Data to the Point of Decision Making	Provide the Proper Tools	Create Organizational Will
Key Elements	**Key Elements**	**Key Elements**	**Key Elements**

• Empowered people
 	
• Cross Functional Metrics
 	
• Clearly define business processes
	• Knowledge Repository for Exception procedures
	
	• Integrated data repository to support Supply Chain
	
	• Rapid Data Access
		• Adaptable over Time
		
		• Integrated with Desktop
		
		• Simple but NOT Simplistic
		  • Mathematical Optimization
		  • Statistical Analysis/tools
		  • Simulation
		  • Expert Systems
			• Management Support
			
			• Training
			
			• Users involved in Design
			
			• Rapid "design and use" cycles

Simply defining the rules and delivering the data is not enough because each new decision is not exactly the same as the previous one. Participants must be able to employ the necessary tools to manipulate this data. Not all tools are needed all the time, but the tools need to be available when needed.

Lastly, sustainable change requires management participation and support. Without active and constant support, improvements tend to fade over time.

Functional Component Deployment Mitigates the Risk of Software Implementation

Early supply chain planning software addressed specific point solutions. Very few companies had the notion of an integrated supply chain. Most regarded the supply chain as a series of process steps like forecasting, capacity balancing, inventory planning, and scheduling. In part, this was because the software offered by vendors addressed these specific areas separately.

The expectation was that companies would acquire and deploy each process step in turn, with the output of one feeding the next. Forecasting software would generate a demand statement that was used in capacity balancing, and the results might be run through a materials requirements planning (MRP) engine to generate component and raw material requirements. Inventory planning was confined to setting safety stock targets and scheduling was a short term local optimization activity.

Functional Component deployment takes a more people centered view. It recognizes that each process step in supply chain planning requires certain capabilities to support decision making. Some of these capabilities cut across the traditional supply chain process steps and software should target all the planners who need a particular capability.

As an example, the ability to gather data from multiple sources and access it readily is something that the scheduler needs. But it is also a capability that the S&OP planner, the demand planner, and others in the supply chain need. Traditional software would provide this capability within the software for demand planning, scheduling, and supply planning "modules," but could provide it in potentially different ways. In addition, the capability would not be available for use until the software addressing a process step was completely deployed.

The distinguishing feature of the functional component architecture is that each component (like quick data access) can simultaneously support a number of supply chain planning process steps. It can also be deployed and used independently. Why is this important?

In a world of tight margins and operating challenges, companies need a fast return on their investments. More importantly, companies need to budget the time and cost of their software implementation reliably because the benefits associated with software implementations are usually achieved after the system is in place.

In our experience, software with the functional component architecture is particularly suited to the evolutionary approach and is much more successful than the "big-bang" approach for improving supply chain planning. The functional component architecture provides a means to limit the scope of software deployment while addressing the needs of multiple planners. It provides the biggest" bang for the buck." It leverages the software deployment so that it improves a number of areas in supply chain planning simultaneously.

An evolutionary approach addresses not just *what* is to be done but also *how* to do it. It mitigates the risk to the business because each step is limited in scope and can be monitored independently. Every software deployment encounters unexpected delays or difficulties. With an evolutionary approach, the time between implementation steps can be extended if these are encountered. In an evolutionary approach, the emphasis is on getting better, rather than implementing the perfect solution.

To implement an evolutionary approach, the improvements have to be introduced in small increments. At each increment, processes are modified and the software required to implement the processes is introduced. Practically, this can only be done if the business receives some value from the change. Hence the change has to be visible and measurable.

Software that has the functional component architecture is suited for an evolutionary approach because it allows you to deliver, test and institutionalize a "complete" solution for a limited business need. While the deployment effort for each functional component is limited, the capability provides benefits across the organization. As each change is demonstrated and used, it creates its own momentum for changing both the business process and the software.

Early Software

Early supply chain planning software addressed specific point solutions. In the 90's, companies began to see the value of integrated data and integrated processes. Much of this was driven by the availability of ERP software and the need to minimize the costs associated with managing data and software systems.

Supply chain planning software vendors responded to this by expanding their footprint. Many of the early scheduling solutions like I2 and Chesapeake acquired companies that extended their reach into demand forecasting, warehousing, and purchasing. These first generation offerings were loosely integrated collections of point solutions, often integrated only from a marketing perspective.

These early solutions were developed specifically for one or two customers, and then commercialized for the market. The software contained assumptions and business processes associated with the first customers. Implementation was difficult because of the customization that was needed for each new customer. Often the integration of data between components of the planning software was as difficult as the integration with external systems.

To support the exchange of information, supply chain applications are required to get data from, and provide data to, many users. The first generation SCP solutions were not well suited for supporting multiple users, distributing information, desktop reporting, and other capabilities required to support modern collaborative planning. Many of these first generation tools are based on a proprietary database and proprietary report writers. In some cases, creating suitable reports involves custom programming.

First generation SCP solutions normally provide a mechanism to export and import data, usually using text (ASCII) files or SQL to interact with external data sources. Our experience shows that the vast majority of failures in production systems occur within the interfaces between the SCP system and the external data sources. These failures tend to occur more often as the interfaces are expanded to accommodate more functionality and increased data visibility.

Companies using first generation SCP solutions are caught in a quandary. The basic tools designed for core supply chain functions like demand management, planning, and schedule management are operational and generally adequate, but are no longer sufficient to support a company's supply chain planning processes by themselves. Efforts to support multiple users with web based tools linking directly into the early SCP solutions have had qualified success. The effort required for setting up and maintaining this infrastructure is significant. Long term supportability and the ongoing cost of the solution continue to be a major concern.

However, the investment in the existing toolset is usually significant enough that direct replacement with a modern system is not an option. Yet maintaining the current systems effectively limits the extent to which they can implement collaborative processes and harvest additional savings.

Modern Software

As modern software evolved, functions which had been customized for each user became standardized. For example, proprietary data storage was replaced by commercial databases, and many optimization algorithms like linear programming were replaced with commercial solvers.

In recent years non-proprietary databases have become capable of handling the large amount of data needed to support many supply chain applications. These databases come with a rich set of connectivity tools that make desktop reporting simple. Increasingly, report creation is seen as an end-user task.

Modern solutions are database centric and often based on Microsoft components, with SQL Server as its foundation. This reduces development costs and allows for more aggressive pricing.

The result is that modern supply chain planning software involves an assembly of software components like algorithmic components, optimization solvers, database access components, and visual components like a Gantt chart. The integration of these components is at the code level.

In addition to the traditional functions, modern Supply Chain Planning systems provide extensions that assist collaboration and promote integration across the supply chain. These include:

- A database to reconcile and manage multiple users working on planning data and enforce access restrictions. To support the expanded requirements, a database paradigm is essential. This allows multiple people to query and report on data.

  A database also simplifies the task of scenario management, like storing and comparing different versions of a plan, and provide many tools like OLAP (On-Line Analytical Processing) that simplify reporting and aggregation.

- A "document and process" repository that is fully integrated with the supply chain software. This repository is designed to contain exception procedures, business process diagrams, transaction flows, and other documents that form the supply chain business processes.

- A monitoring and event flagging system that can warn about potential events in the future. Plans need to be monitored after they are made. Potential challenges need to be identified and the appropriate people notified for resolution.

  It is not sufficient to base the event flagging on just status information, or on things that happened in the past. Planning systems have the data to project into the future and identify risks.

Functional Component Architecture

While using the technology components simplifies the development and reliability of software, it does not reduce the time for implementation because each component cannot be deployed by itself. However, it does mean that SCP software at its basic level has become somewhat generic because most modern software uses the same commercially offered technology components.

Lately, some software vendors have extended the notion of component based software by creating a layer of functional components that address needs across supply chain processes. These functionality components are built around the business capability that a user needs. They are different from the technology components because each of these SCP components combines elements of database access, optimization, and the user interface. The key advantage of course is that each SCP component can be deployed by itself and immediately provide benefits across the supply chain.

Let's look at how the notion of functional components through an example.

Scheduling Example

The Scheduler's Dilemma

The Scheduler has a difficult job because he or she has to deal with many people who have conflicting objectives. The job is further complicated because the scheduler has to gather a bunch of information from different sources. The Scheduler spends most of the time gathering the right information, like the current status of the shop floor, the demand in the next few weeks, the shutdown schedule, the projected receipts of raw materials, and so on.

One of the things that she needs from a software solution is to make her job easier, by automating the data collection.

The next challenge that the Scheduler has is that the data from many sources is not necessarily consistent. Therefore, she needs the tools to analyze data and point out inconsistencies. She needs to identify inconsistencies like the following:

- The schedule has an operation for 200 for a product, but the company is already swimming in inventory for that product.

- There is a product scheduled, but there is no inventory of a component required for producing it.

- We are missing orders are for product xyz.

The scheduler would also like the ability to store and maintain data which is needed in scheduling but is not available from any other system. Rather than keep it in a proprietary Excel workbook or on paper, the scheduler would like to make this accessible.

Even if the Scheduler knows the problems, he or she can only react to the NEXT problem. It is difficult to see the consequences of the changes a Scheduler makes without a tool to quickly show the effects of changes. The Scheduler may well be creating difficulties in the future, but she does not know because there is no time to evaluate things well for a reasonable length of time. The best that she can do is worry about the next major event like a shutdown or demand spike. Therefore, the scheduler needs to represent the current schedule in the software and show the impact of a manual change so that she will have a longer time horizon.

The consequences of the changes also need to be consistent with the business objectives as represented by the S&OP. Otherwise, the schedule becomes a reflection of who shouts the loudest.

The Scheduler has to deal with conflicting objectives from people in the organization. The marketing people always want to react to their needs, and meanwhile the manufacturing guys are complaining about schedule changes. To help the Scheduler get some of these conflicts resolved, we need a quantitative framework to measure how good a schedule is.

The objective is to quantify only those elements that can be supported with data. Of course we can't quantify everything, and it is not the intent to, but at least we can try to list the quantitative things like number of orders missed, setup-costs, and so on, and provide a way of costing out the schedule. The advantage of this is that the Scheduler will be able to compare the quantitative attributes of two schedules. So now, if marketing wants to make a change, the Scheduler is able to calculate if it is going to cost $50,000 or $2,000. This will let the Scheduler channel her energy to fight the important battles rather than fighting all of them.

The scheduler is always harried and never has enough time. To alleviate this, it would be nice to reduce the repetitive work she does in maintaining the schedule. There also may be better ways of handling some of the tasks like lot sizing, and sequencing, and resource usage. This involves identifying opportunities to optimize and to implement these opportunities.

What the Scheduler Needs

The business capabilities (or functional components) that a scheduler needs can be summarized as:

1. The capability to gather the data needed by the scheduler to do scheduling in one place. This data needs to be up-to-date and easily accessible.

2. The capability to identify internal data inconsistencies.

3. The capability to represent the schedule in a tool and show the impact when the scheduler makes manual changes.

4. The capability to compare the schedule with the S&OP plan.

5. The capability to quantify the relevant costs of a schedule.

6. The capability to automate and optimize routine activities that consume the scheduler's time.

Functional Component Deployment

A similar narrative can identify the capabilities or functional components needed by other planners. For illustrative purposes, we have summarized some of these in the table below.

	Demand Planner	Supply Planner	Inventory Planner
1	The ability to gather the required data in one place	The ability to gather the required data in one place	The ability to gather the required data in one place
2	The ability to analyze the data and detect internal inconsistencies	The ability to analyze the data and detect internal inconsistencies	The ability to analyze the data and detect internal inconsistencies
3	The ability to identify variability in the demand and select a suitable forecasting procedure	Modeling capability to quantitatively represent the supply chain operations	Modeling capability to quantitatively represent the variability in the supply chain
4	The ability to manage changes and overrides	Optimization engines to evaluate and select the best alternative	Procedures to calculate appropriate amount of safety stocks, cycle stocks and other buffer stock.
5	The ability to aggregate and disaggregate the forecast	Capability to override the plan and measure the impact.	A suitable replenishment engine to position inventory in the supply chain
6	The ability to consolidate multiple inputs into a single demand statement		
7	The ability to disseminate the plan	The ability to disseminate the plan	The ability to disseminate the plan
8	The ability to measure and monitor the plan	The ability to measure and monitor the plan	The ability to measure and monitor the plan

The goal of functional component deployment is to improve the entire supply chain organization one step at a time. Rather than implement each capability for a process step, this approach identifies the common capabilities or business functions and deploys them across the organization. Let us take the example of "The ability to disseminate the plan."

In the functional deployment approach, this might be accomplished by establishing a central data base which connects directly with the existing spreadsheets used by the various business processes. Access to the central warehouse is then provided through the database using standard desktop tools. This simple change does not disrupt the existing work processes, but provides some immediate benefits:

- It consolidates all the plans into a single repository which can be shared.

- The single repository acts as the catalyst for the individual planners to keep their portion of the plan updated.

- The central repository prepares the organization for metrics across different functional areas.

- It provides the beginning of a framework for collaboration.

Similarly, the same functional component that is able to display and analyze data from a variety of sources may be deployed simultaneously for all planners. Of course, certain functional components are restricted to one or two process steps. For example, the demand planner's solution will contain functional components like the ability to generate a statistical forecast, aggregate and disaggregate forecasts, and so on.

Common Functional Components

Modern supply chain planning is about making consistent decisions under uncertainty. This means that certain core capabilities must be available to all planners.

Access to Data

The common myth is that data access is all about making the ERP data accessible. This is an important part, but not sufficient by itself because the ERP systems essentially keep data for things that have happened and not for things that are going to happen. ERP systems are notoriously difficult to configure so that they keep versions of future plans, data that does not directly affect transactions, and unstructured data. They are designed to provide accounting data integrity. They need to make sure that costs add up consistently, but are not concerned about how the costs are allocated. For example, it does not matter to the ERP system if product transition costs are allocated to the asset or to the product, as long as all the relevant costs like energy and waste are accounted for. For optimizing the planning processes, the proper allocation of costs matters.

To support the planners, the ERP data needs to be provided in a way that the planners can analyze, aggregate, and manipulate the data to support decision making. Most companies have found that a central planning database with a relational structure is helpful to support this. This central repository normally contains ERP data, versions of excel spreadsheets that the planners use, exception procedures, and versions of future plans.

Desktop Integration

Planners use desktop tools as a matter of course for very specific analysis or to present and communicate data. While the specific view of the data is not that important, it is critical that planners use up-to-date and consistent data. By providing a single planning data repository, together with the tools to communicate with desktop tools, the organization can facilitate data sharing and the dissemination of plans like the forecast, S&OP plan, and the schedule. Often, this can be provided without changing the individual work processes of the planners, but by simply providing additional tools to link their existing planning tools to a data repository.

At a minimum, desktop integration provides the ability to exchange data between the central repository and the desktop tools, manage versions of different plans or spreadsheets, and the data security features to support appropriate dissemination of information.

Supply Chain Metrics

To facilitate quantitative planning, the supply chain has to be monitored. Greatest benefit is obtained by monitoring the entire supply chain and institutionalizing metrics that cut across processes. Rather than monitoring the accuracy of the forecast, it is better to monitor the number of schedule changes caused by an inaccurate forecast. This provides a direct incentive to improve the individual processes. Deployment of this functionality is something that can be done across the supply chain and does not have to wait until all the different sub-processes in the supply chain have been restructured and optimized.

Collaboration Infrastructure

Collaboration between planners and other groups in a company cannot be enforced. No system will automatically create a collaborative planning environment. At the same time, the absence of a system infrastructure will inhibit the ability of planners and others to work cooperatively.

At the minimum, a collaborative infrastructure must provide and present relevant data, allow for inputs easily, store the inputs as they are entered, be able to consolidate multiple inputs, and measure results and plans against the inputs. In every supply chain, inputs from different groups are being provided, often through emails, phone calls, and spreadsheets mailed from one person to another. A collaborative infrastructure can be set up to support the existing information exchanges without waiting for the individual processes to be rationalized. This can always be extended to include additional data exchanges.

Conclusion

By deploying certain common functional components before embarking on improving the individual supply chain planning processes, a company can mitigate its deployment risk. The common components help to elicit support from the planners by improving capabilities and providing tangible value to the business. This strategy leaves the hard part of process improvements and changing work processes to a later stage. By making the data accessible and providing some rudimentary tools to the planners first, it makes the job of changing work processes easier because it demonstrates tangible progress quickly.

Architecture for Tactical Supply Chain Planning

Early Supply Chain Planning (SCP) Systems evolved from Material Requirement Planning (MRP) software. These systems had a clear hierarchical organization with demand forecasting, tactical planning, scheduling clearly differentiated. Many companies attempted to implement a sequential process that generated a forecast once a month which was then passed to planning, and scheduling was expected to use the monthly plan to make and distribute products during the month.

In practice, the environment is rarely static enough to support a process that is defined rigidly in this manner. Because the business environment keeps changing, orders rarely match the forecast, and manufacturing cannot operate consistently, feedback loops were added to the basic sequential process.

Eventually, a consensus emerged that the basic monthly cycle of forecasting, capacity planning and scheduling had to be supported with a constant update of data.

Keeping data up to date is facilitated by a central planning repository. While a typical ERP system contains much of the data used for tactical planning, in our experience, a separate and distinct planning data repository is necessary because planning and transaction systems are fundamentally different.

1. To maintain data integrity, the ERP system preserves transactional integrity through tight control access and administration. A planning system is more concerned with data consistency and the ability to support "what ifs." In addition, the planning data may consist of a number of temporary scenarios or "plans" for the future. These scenarios are used for analysis and comparison and they might not be stored for more than a day or two.

2. While it may be a desirable goal to keep all data required for planning in the ERP system, this is never the case because the planning environment needs to be more dynamic than the transaction environment. There may be a need to categorize products temporarily, or create hierarchies that are different from the ERP. For example, some ERP systems attach the sales person to the order. The sales person remains attached to the order even if territories are reassigned or sales persons leave. While this is useful for record keeping purposes, planning may want to look how product and customer combinations are allocated to the current sales staff.

3. In many organizations, key planning data like transition times and manufacturing characteristics are kept on spreadsheets or systems not directly connected to the ERP system. It is appropriate that these are not stored in the ERP system because its role is to ensure that costs are recorded and allocated consistently. Optimization of costs is never the goal of the ERP system.

Current "Accepted" Practice

The data that is normally exposed through the planning data repository is illustrated below. The key is that any and all data that also exists in the ERP and other systems is maintained in the ERP and in the other systems.

Planning Data Repository

Single Data Repository to facilitate
- **Security and Data Management,**
- **User access and role based security**
- **ERP data interchange**

- **Demand**
- Orders,
- Shipments,
- Invoices
- **Static Data**
- Facilities, Rates, Routes
- Products, Bill -of- Materials, Recipes, Formulas,
- Transport Constraints,
- Manufacturing Constraints
- Qualification Schedules
- Staffing Constraints,
- **Current Status**
- Inventory
- Production Status
- Projected receipts
- WIP
- Transport/rail car status
- **Costs and Priorities**
- Customer segmentation
- Transition / ingredient costs
- Distribution cost
- Contracts, price
- Inventory targets

Modern planning systems almost inevitably support a demand forecasting or demand planning process. While there are some advocates of "no forecasting," it is generally accepted that at some level, a company has to predict its material requirements. Forecasting may be at the final product level or for a major ingredient that is purchased depending on the manufacturing lead time. In either case, the process of coming up with a statement of projected demand is best done through collaboration with all the stakeholders. The diagram below provides a generic view of how such a process is supported.

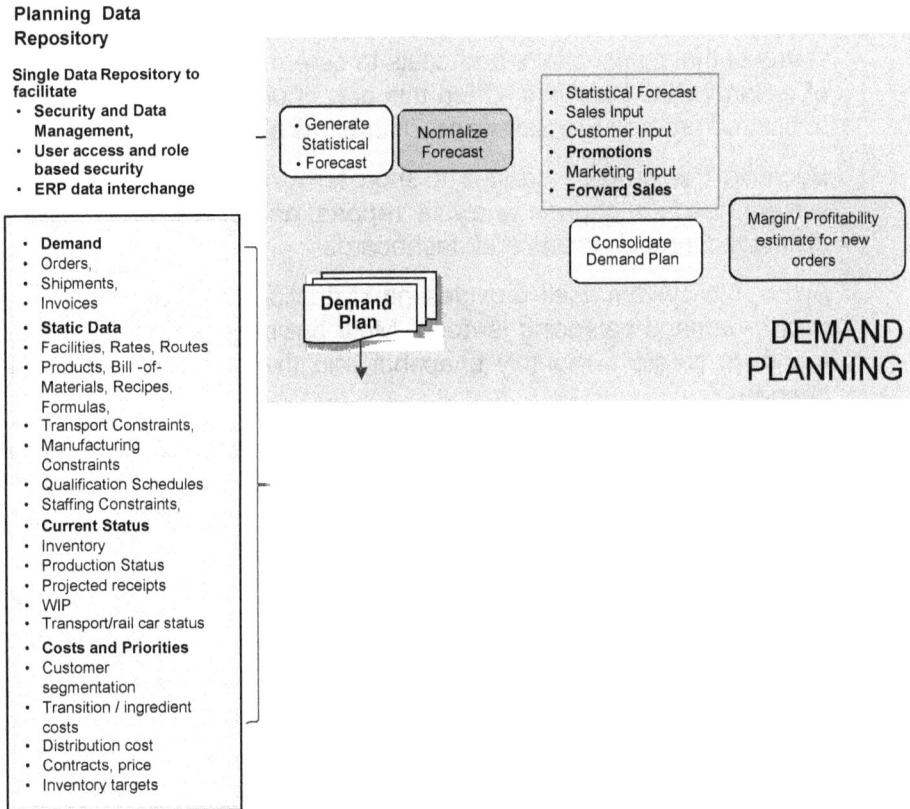

Planning Data Repository

Single Data Repository to facilitate
- **Security and Data Management,**
- **User access and role based security**
- **ERP data interchange**

- **Demand**
- Orders,
- Shipments,
- Invoices
- **Static Data**
- Facilities, Rates, Routes
- Products, Bill -of- Materials, Recipes, Formulas,
- Transport Constraints,
- Manufacturing Constraints
- Qualification Schedules
- Staffing Constraints,
- **Current Status**
- Inventory
- Production Status
- Projected receipts
- WIP
- Transport/rail car status
- **Costs and Priorities**
- Customer segmentation
- Transition / ingredient costs
- Distribution cost
- Contracts, price
- Inventory targets

- Generate Statistical
- Forecast

Normalize Forecast

- Statistical Forecast
- Sales Input
- Customer Input
- **Promotions**
- Marketing input
- **Forward Sales**

Consolidate Demand Plan

Margin/ Profitability estimate for new orders

Demand Plan

DEMAND PLANNING

Data from the planning repository is used to generate a preliminary statistical forecast. This is exposed to the stakeholders including sales and marketing. Their input and potential adjustments are gathered and then consolidated through a structured process to come up with a single statement of projected demand. Typically, this is done once a month, but there is no system restriction to limit the frequency with which the demand plan is generated.

At a daily level, the projected demand is updated with the current orders to reflect the latest picture of demand. Often this process is called forecast netting. It may be a simple process of subtracting the monthly orders from the forecast, or a more sophisticated process that takes into account the distribution of orders within a forecast period.

Supply planning utilizes the latest demand plan, the resource data, the current status of the supply chain, and costs to determine the best short term course of action for the business. Often this part of planning is supported through a structured process like Sales and Operations planning.

Because this process creates a short term roadmap for the business, the system needs to support analysis, reports, and diagnostics. Often these are distributed through charts and dashboards.

Again, the system itself provides no restriction (nor should it) of how often supply-demand balancing is done. Most businesses do this at least once a month to create a monthly snapshot and then modify it as circumstances change.

The supply planning process generates the guidance to daily changes to the schedule. It may also generate targets for order promising or restrictions for the Available-to-Promise (ATP) process. At the same time, it needs to know the current commitments which include the orders, as well as the projected manufacturing and distribution schedules. Without this, and supply/demand planning is done in a vacuum. The targets and the schedules are more often than not kept in the central database. Depending on the degree of automation required, the schedules may actually be input directly from the ERP and are sometimes referred to as production orders or released production orders.

Planning Data Repository

Single Data Repository to facilitate
- **Security and Data Management,**
- **User access and role based security**
- ERP data interchange

- **Demand**
- Orders,
- Shipments,
- Invoices
- **Static Data**
- Facilities, Rates, Routes
- Products, Bill -of- Materials, Recipes, Formulas,
- Transport Constraints,
- Manufacturing Constraints
- Qualification Schedules
- Staffing Constraints,
- **Current Status**
- Inventory
- Production Status
- Projected receipts
- WIP
- Transport/rail car status
- **Costs and Priorities**
- Customer segmentation
- Transition / ingredient costs
- Distribution cost
- Contracts, price
- Inventory targets

DEMAND PLANNING

- •Generate Statistical
- • Forecast

Normalize Forecast

- Statistical Forecast
- Sales Input
- Customer Input
- **Promotions**
- Marketing input
- **Forward Sales**

Consolidate Demand Plan

Margin/ Profitability estimate for new orders

Demand Plan

Business Demand Projections

SUPPLY PLANNING

Supply - Demand Balancing

- **Supply Chain Analysis**
- **Scenario Management**
- **S&OP reports**
- **Financial reports**
- **Supply/Demand Diagnostics**

Raw Material Planning

Staffing and Capacity Planning

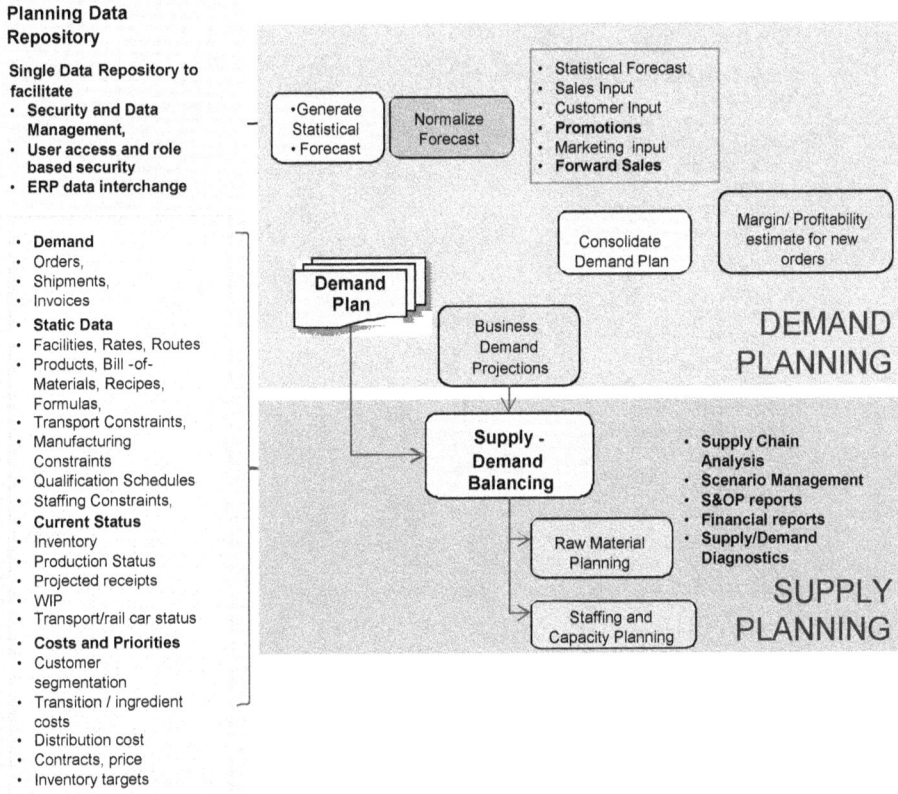

The targets generated by the supply-demand balancing process are used to guide the daily planning transactions. This may include manufacturing scheduling, distribution, the ATP process and short term inventory reallocation decisions. Much of the data used at this level depends on the business in question and is omitted from this overview.

Planning Data Repository

Single Data Repository to facilitate
- **Security and Data Management,**
- **User access and role based security**
- **ERP data interchange**

- **Demand**
- Orders,
- Shipments,
- Invoices
- **Static Data**
- Facilities, Rates, Routes
- Products, Bill-of-Materials, Recipes, Formulas,
- Transport Constraints,
- Manufacturing Constraints
- Qualification Schedules
- Staffing Constraints,
- **Current Status**
- Inventory
- Production Status
- Projected receipts
- WIP
- Transport/rail car status
- **Costs and Priorities**
- Customer segmentation
- Transition / ingredient costs
- Distribution cost
- Contracts, price
- Inventory targets

DEMAND PLANNING

- •Generate Statistical
- • Forecast

- Statistical Forecast
- Sales Input
- Customer Input
- New product plans
- Marketing input

Demand Plan

- •Consolidate
- •Demand Plan

SUPPLY PLANNING

- •Combine Orders
- •with Forecasts

- **Supply Chain Analysis**
- **Scenario Management**
- **S&OP reports**
- **Financial reports**
- **Supply/Demand Diagnostics**

- •Supply-Demand Balancing

Targets

SCHEDULING

Schedules

Finite Scheduling

- Detect fluctuations in inventory, demand and production status and adjust the schedule
- Inventory Planning
- Simulate scheduling and production to support supply planning, and manage distribution

- **Alerts**
- **Review schedule and inventory trace**
- **Schedule editing**
- **Schedule release**
- **Sales control and supply maps**

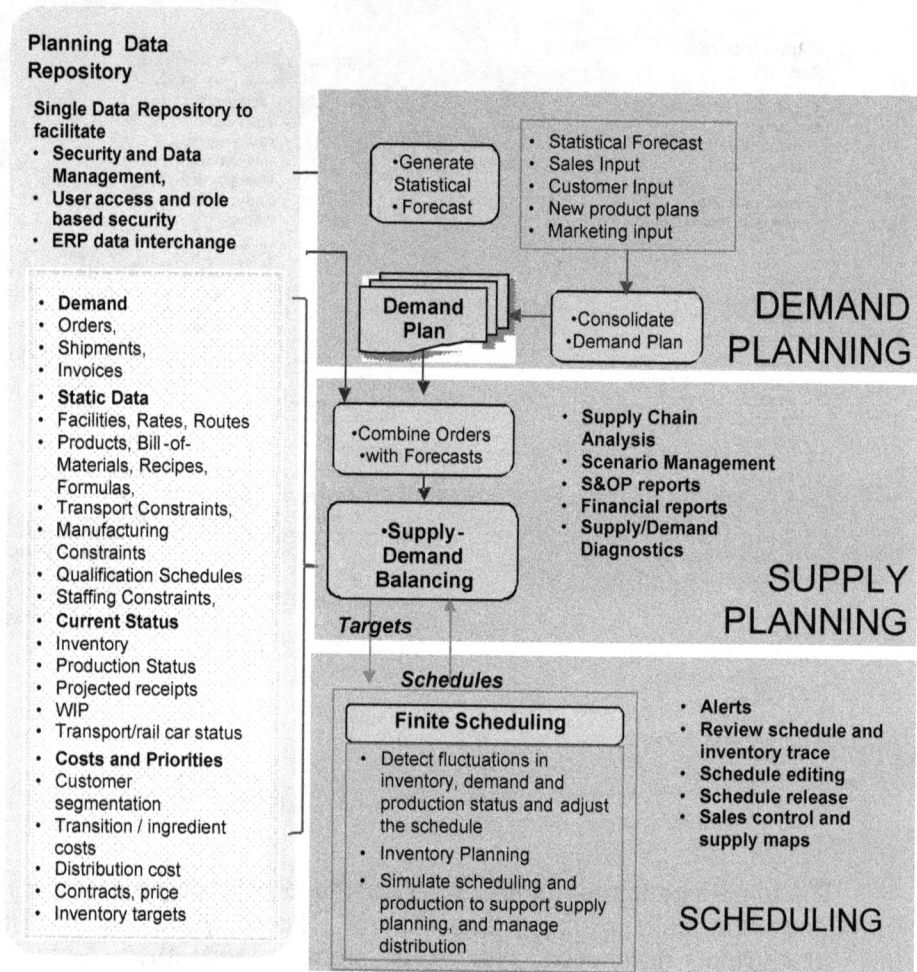

The output of this process may include alerts, manufacturing order releases, supply maps to guide the shipment dispatch and other short term supply chain activities. The key difference between the scheduling step and the supply demand balancing step is that scheduling is more concerned with "feasibility" or making things doable in the short term, and less concerned with overall optimization. Overall optimization is generally done at the supply-demand balancing step and enforced at the scheduling level through targets.

With a few variations, the architecture outlined above is generally accepted as the "best practice" or at least the accepted practice for supporting tactical planning.

Supporting a Dynamic Environment

While the architecture described above is suitable for many companies, the current business environment requires that changes in the environment be incorporated into the planning process quickly. At the same time, a plan is just that – a plan - and it does no good to create a plan if you change it in response to every perturbation.

Most companies can live with a plan that is created once a month. This is a natural planning cycle because most financial and accounting reporting is done with this frequency. There is a strong argument that operational planning should be synchronized with the financial operations.

For companies with a heavy process focus, this is a significant issue because the time required to react is usually determined by the flexibility of the assets at the beginning of the manufacturing process. These assets are usually expensive and changing schedules quickly is either not feasible or costly in both time and material. The supply chain can operate much more efficiently if changes in demand are communicated without delay because this gives the manufacturing process more time to react.

Recently, some companies are looking at planning in a slightly different way in an attempt to divorce updates to the plan from a rigid monthly cycle. Rather than thinking of the tactical demand and supply plans as the output of a process, they think of these as entities that are evergreen. The current demand and supply plan are maintained in the planning data repository, as are any changes to the input data like sales and marketing input, manufacturing upsets and other external deviations from the plan. These inputs are not entered on any cycle but are updated when they occur.

Three types of changes are monitored.

1. The planning database is constantly updated with changes from sales, customers, and customer service representatives.

2. It is also updated with the manufacturing performance to the plan.

3. Plan assumptions like raw material spot prices, petroleum prices, the financial health of key customers, or in the case of the food industry, recalls or health related events are also updated in the repository.

These changes and deviations from the monthly plan are continuously monitored. Normally the summary of changes is automatically distributed through dashboards and warning messages.

In addition to the normal planning cycle, there is a separate review process for changes that exceed predefined thresholds.

Let's take the case of a customer that seeks chapter 11 bankruptcy protections. If this is not a significant customer (as defined by a threshold value for revenue) then a routine warning message is communicated. If this is a significant customer, then it might affect the supply plan for the products that the customer buys and a review process to evaluate the significance of this event is initiated. The goal of the review process is to determine if the event can be handled by changes within the current plan, or if a new plan has to be created. This review process cannot be automated. It is usually assisted by a system that can simulate changes against the current plan, but it cannot be totally automated because the changes required depend on when in the month the event occurs, the business climate, and other considerations.

In our example, if the customer is a large one and has taken most of his forecast for the month, then the current plan would likely not be changed but the information would be used in the next planning cycle. If significant shipments are still scheduled, then the situation might be handled through a direct intervention at the tactical scheduling level to delay the shipments until additional credit checks are complete.

On the other hand, if significant manufacturing resources are yet to be allocated to meet this customer's demand, then it might indeed be reasonable to revise the current monthly plan. Where and how to intervene cannot be automated, but the process to deal with changes can and should be.

Planning Data Repository

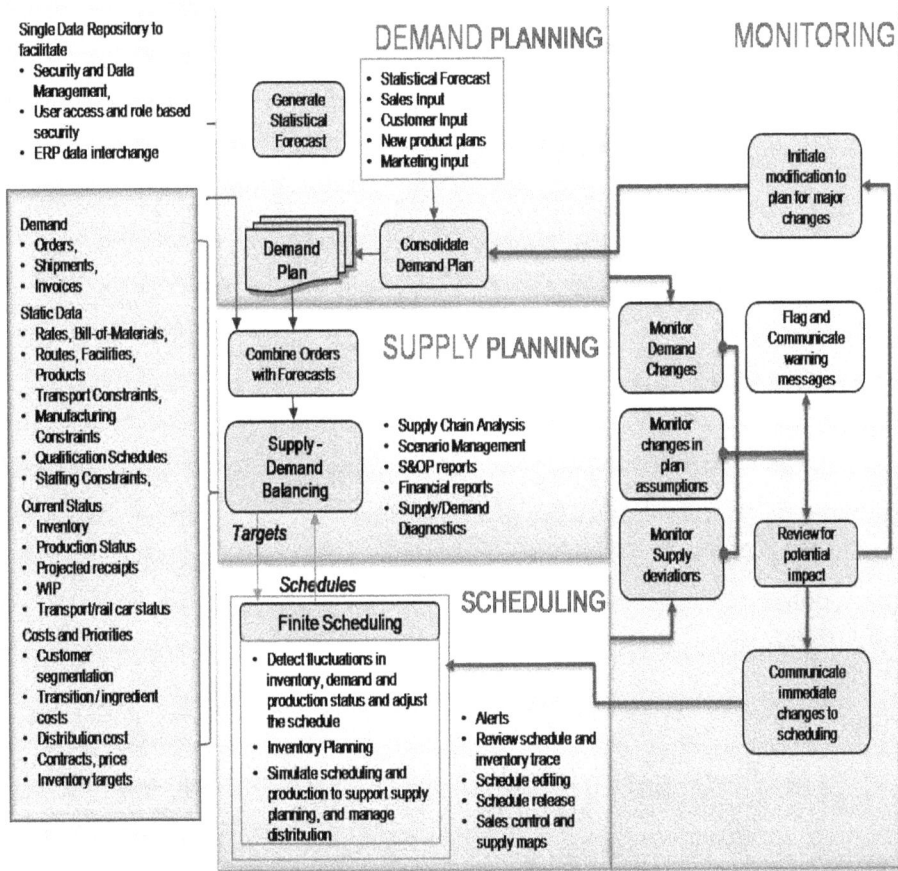

Single Data Repository to facilitate
- Security and Data Management,
- User access and role based security
- ERP data interchange

Demand
- Orders,
- Shipments,
- Invoices

Static Data
- Rates, Bill-of-Materials,
- Routes, Facilities, Products
- Transport Constraints,
- Manufacturing Constraints
- Qualification Schedules
- Staffing Constraints,

Current Status
- Inventory
- Production Status
- Projected receipts
- WIP
- Transport/rail car status

Costs and Priorities
- Customer segmentation
- Transition / ingredient costs
- Distribution cost
- Contracts, price
- Inventory targets

DEMAND PLANNING

Generate Statistical Forecast

- Statistical Forecast
- Sales Input
- Customer Input
- New product plans
- Marketing input

Demand Plan

Consolidate Demand Plan

SUPPLY PLANNING

Combine Orders with Forecasts

Supply-Demand Balancing

Targets

- Supply Chain Analysis
- Scenario Management
- S&OP reports
- Financial reports
- Supply/Demand Diagnostics

Schedules

SCHEDULING

Finite Scheduling

- Detect fluctuations in inventory, demand and production status and adjust the schedule
- Inventory Planning
- Simulate scheduling and production to support supply planning, and manage distribution

- Alerts
- Review schedule and inventory trace
- Schedule editing
- Schedule release
- Sales control and supply maps

MONITORING

Initiate modification to plan for major changes

Monitor Demand Changes

Flag and Communicate warning messages

Monitor changes in plan assumptions

Monitor Supply deviations

Review for potential impact

Communicate immediate changes to scheduling

The Ongoing Challenge in Semiconductors

Creating an Enterprise-Wide Detailed Supply Chain Plan

By Ken Fordyce

The Decision Framework

In the mid 1980s, Karl Kempf of Intel and Gary Sullivan of IBM independently proposed that planning, scheduling, and dispatch decisions across an enterprise's demand-supply network were best viewed as a series of information flows and decision points organized in a hierarchy or set of decision tiers (Sullivan 1990). This remains the most powerful method to view supply chains in enterprises with complex activities.

Recently, Kempf (2004) eloquently rephrased this approach in today's supply chain terminology, and Sullivan (2005) added a second dimension based on supply chain activities to create the grid below to classify decision support in demand-supply networks. The row dimension is decision tier and the column dimension is responsible unit. The area called global or enterprise-wide central planning falls within this grid.

Demand/Supply Network Planning, Scheduling, and Dispatch (PSD) Activity Areas and Decision Tiers

		Demand / Supply Activity Areas		
		Demand Statement Creation	Enterprise-wide Global View	Enterprise Subunits (Manufacturing, Distribution, Retail)
Decision Tiers	Tier 1: Strategic			
	Tier 2: Tactical			
	Tier 3: Operational "Daily"			
	Tier 3.5: Sub-daily Guidance			
	Tier 4 Response			

Demand-supply network (or supply chain) decisions in the semiconductor industry typically fall into one of four decision tiers (row dimension): strategic, tactical, operational, and response (dispatch). The categories are based on the planning horizon, the apparent width of the opportunity window, and the level of precision required in supporting the information.

The first decision tier, **strategic scheduling**, is typically driven by the lead time required for business planning, resource acquisition, and new product introduction. This tier can often be viewed in two parts: **very long-term** and **long-term**. Here, decision makers are concerned with a set of decisions that have consequences three months to seven years into the future. Issues considered include, but are not limited to, what markets the firm will be in, general availability of tooling and workers, major process changes, risk assessment of changes in demand for existing products, required or expected incremental improvements in the production process, lead times for additional tooling, manpower and planning.

The second tier, **tactical scheduling**, deals with consequences the company faces in the next week to six months. Estimates are made of yields, cycle times, and binning percentages. Permissible material substitutions are identified. Decisions are made about scheduling starts or releases into the manufacturing line (committing available capacity to new starts). Delivery dates are estimated for firm orders, available "outs" by time buckets are estimated for bulk products, and daily going rates (DGR) for schedule-driven products are set. The order/release plan is generated or regenerated, and (customer-requested) reschedules are negotiated.

The third tier, **operational scheduling**, deals with the execution and achievement of a weekly plan. Shipments are made, serviceability levels are measured, and recovery actions are taken. Optimal capacity consumption and product output are computed.

The fourth tier, **real-time response system**, addresses the problems of the next hour to a few weeks by responding to conditions as they emerge in real time. It also accommodates variances from availability assumed in the plan creation and commitment phases. Within the demand-supply network, real time response is often found in two predominant areas: manufacturing dispatch (which assigns lots to tools) and order commitment (available to promise, or ATP). In manufacturing dispatch scheduling (DS), decisions concern monitoring and controlling of the actual manufacturing flow and instructing the operator what to do next to achieve current manufacturing goals. The goal of most ATP applications is to provide a commit date to a customer order as quickly as possible. Although it may not respond in real time, its goal is to modify the current match between assets and demand to provide a real-time commit to an order placed by a customer.

Within semiconductor manufacturing, the decisions made across the tiers are typically handled by groups with one of three responsibilities: establishing product demand, maintaining an enterprise wide global view of the demand-supply network, and ensuring that subunits (such as manufacturing location, vendor, warehouse, etc.) are operating efficiently. Although ideally all planning would be central, in practice the level of complexity precludes this. Capacity or tool planning is a good example. At the enterprise level, capacity is modeled at some level of aggregation, typically viewing a tool set as a single capacity point. At the factory level, each tool, or potentially each chamber in a tool, is modeled.

Basics of Enterprise Wide End to End Central Planning

The activity of concern in this paper, called "enterprise wide end to end central planning," falls into the second column in Sullivan's grid (enterprise wide global view) and straddles the rows: strategic, tactical, and operational. This planning activity, which is a key requirement for successfully managing operations in any manufacturing industry, involves the coordination of supply and demand (current and future). In large scale manufacturing systems such as semiconductor, this planning activity must handle the dual challenges of scope (complexity) and scale (size).

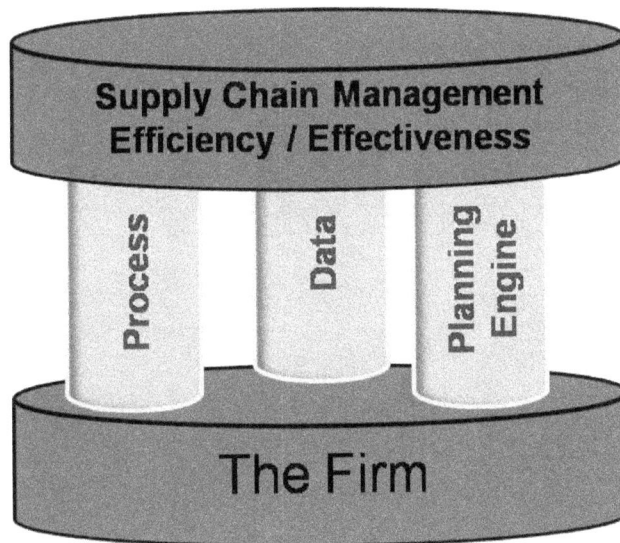

In its simplest form, supply chain planning combines three "basic pillars":

- Business processes and organizational structure;

- Data collection and storage mechanisms; and

- Analytical or modeling methods to execute a planning cycle.

A planning cycle typically consists of the steps described in the table below.

1.	Create a demand statement.
2.	Gather and project assets to a decision point.
3.	Create an enterprise wide end to end central plan by matching current and future assets with current and future demand to generate. . . • A projected supply linked with exit demand including projecting supply without demand, capacity utilization, and pegging. • Synchronization signals across the enterprise including starts (or manufacturing releases), target outs, due dates, ship plans, stocking levels, lot priorities, planned substitutions, capacity utilization, etc.

Typically this is an iterative process that consists of a set of model runs under different settings, such as

- *with and without capacity*
- *with and without new projected supply*
- *with and without new forecasted demand*

Where different runs occur at different times during the week.

4.	Execute the plan.
	a. Send signals to each core enterprise organization (such as manufacturing, storage, vendors, etc.): • Converting this signal into more detailed guidelines for each organization. • Executing the detailed manufacturing or transport activities.
	b. Send projected supply to ATP which • Handles incoming requests for product. • Makes tradeoffs or reallocation as needed and defined by the business rules.
5.	Repeat

Step 3 is often referred to as the enterprise wide best-can-do (BCD) matching, or the central planning engine (CPE). The core task of the CPE is to deploy modeling methods to match assets with demand across an enterprise to create a projected supply linked with demand and synchronization signals. Assets include, but are not limited to, manufacturing starts (or releases), work in progress (WIP), inventory, purchases, and capacity (manufacturing equipment and manpower). Demands include, but are not limited to, firm orders, forecasted orders, and inventory buffer.

The inputs and outputs of a planning run are shown diagrammatically below

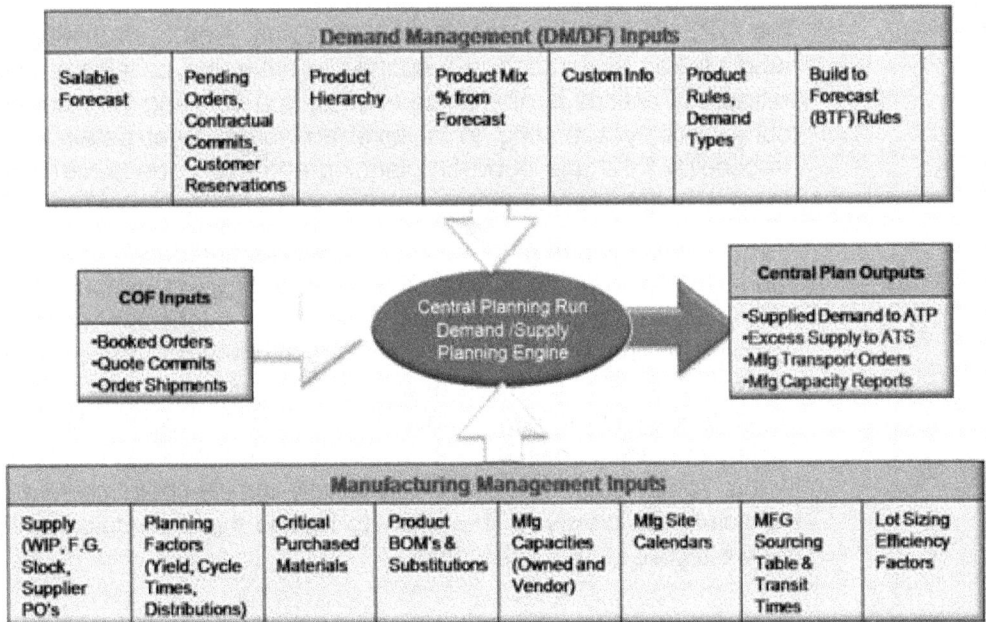

Demand Management (DM/DF) Inputs							
Salable Forecast	Pending Orders, Contractual Commits, Customer Reservations	Product Hierarchy	Product Mix % from Forecast	Custom Info	Product Rules, Demand Types	Build to Forecast (BTF) Rules	

COF Inputs
- Booked Orders
- Quote Commits
- Order Shipments

Central Planning Run Demand /Supply Planning Engine

Central Plan Outputs
- Supplied Demand to ATP
- Excess Supply to ATS
- Mfg Transport Orders
- Mfg Capacity Reports

Manufacturing Management Inputs							
Supply (WIP, F.G. Stock, Supplier PO's	Planning Factors (Yield, Cycle Times, Distributions)	Critical Purchased Materials	Product BOM's & Substitutions	Mfg Capacities (Owned and Vendor)	Mfg Site Calendars	MFG Sourcing Table & Transit Times	Lot Sizing Efficiency Factors

The CPE has four core components which

1. Represent the (potential) material flows in production, business policies, constraints, demand priorities, current locations of asset, etc., and relate all this information to exit demand.

2. Capture asset quantities and parameters (cycle times, yields, binning percentages, etc.).

3. Search and generate a supply chain plan, relate the outcome to demand, and modify the plan to improve the match.

4. Display and explain the results.

The CPE enables an organization to rapidly create an intelligent projected supply linked to demand in response to emerging conditions and based on anticipated actions by the enterprise – it is a planning tool, not an execution tool --- but by operating at lot level and order level detail and having full "traceability," the gap between planning and execution is narrowed as much as possible (and reasonable).

It is true that if you don't have your processes and data in place, the ability of your "CPE" to handle business complexity doesn't matter. However, just having your data and processes in place is no longer enough. Firms now compete on analytics (Davenport 2006) and many of those complexities, such as alternative bill of materials or customer request and commit dates, are core competencies for firms and cannot be "leaned" away without damaging the firm's competitive position. Kempf (2004) observed: "the tradition of referring to this supply-demand network as simply supply-chain grossly understates the actual complexity." The ability to handle these complexities results in a more effective supply chain plan.

Some of the interactions of the CPE with other processes are shown below. This is not an extensive list of supply chain planning functions that a firm has to put in place, but the diagram below illustrates the central role of the CPE in consolidating information and providing a quantitative framework for making decisions.

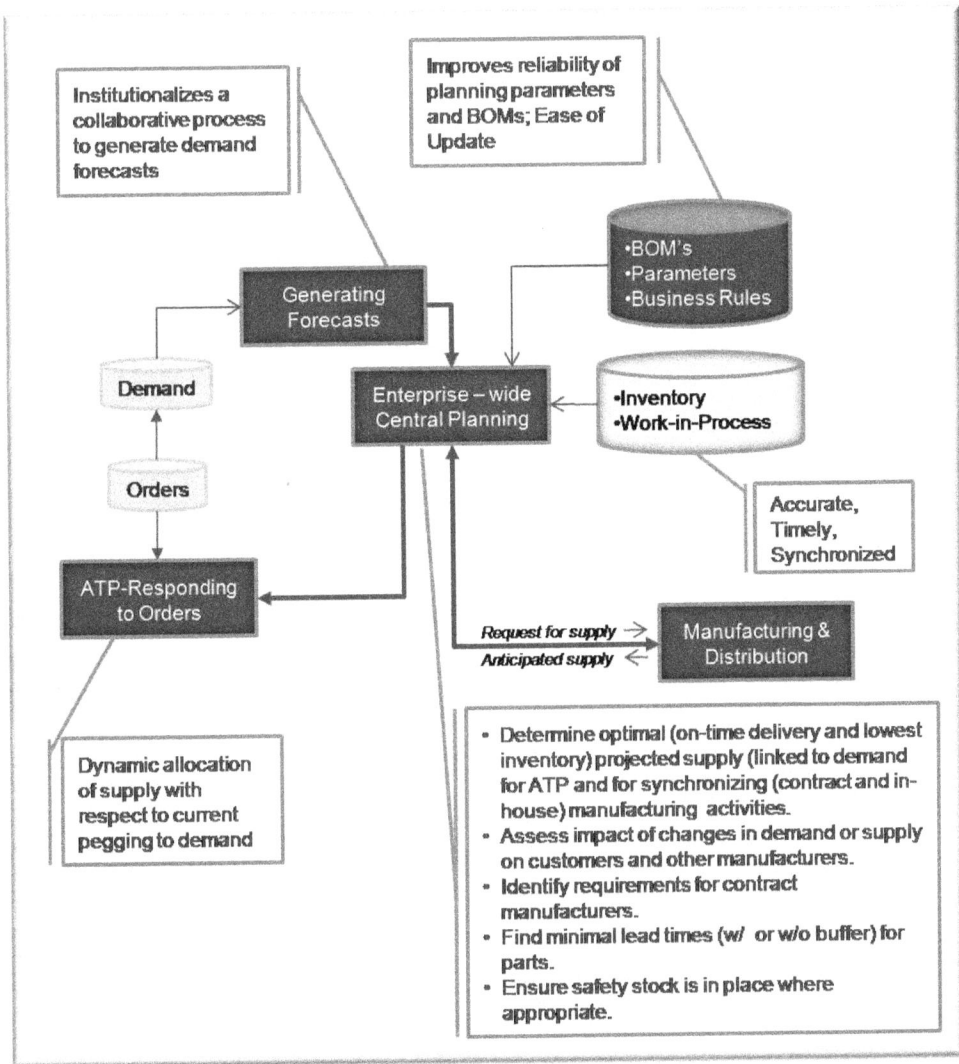

Historical Note

Historically, the concept that an enterprise needs a reasonably tightly coupled central planning process to be successful in the market took hold in the middle 1990s (Shobrys 2003). Within the semiconductor industry, the work at Harris Semiconductor (Leachman et. al. 1996) and Digital Equipment Corporation (Arnzten et al 1995) certainly elevated awareness.

The work by Tayur (1998) noted the growing importance of quantitative models, and the work by Lee (1997), Swaminathan (1998), and Lin (2000) made it clear that real improvements in organizational performance were possible from centralized planning.

To be clear, we are not saying the concept did not exist before and certain businesses had some success at centralized control. Glover et al (1979) produced, at a minimum, a clear ancestor to today's supply chain planning models (including using different models depending on whether strategic or tactical planning was being done). The ten ways that an MRP can fail (Woolsey 1979) still ring true today. Fogarty and Hoffman (1983) identified some core requirements. Duchessi (1987) identified the importance of a feasible production plan and the applicability of knowledge-based techniques to this problem. The papers by Hackman and Leachman (1989), Uzsoy et al (1992, 1994), and Graves et al (1995) clearly identified the emerging need and interest. Norden (1993) articulated the general trend in applying quantitative methods from well-structured operations to the more speculative aspects of strategy and policy formation. In some respects, little is new after Orlicky (1975).

It is clear that the mid 1990s saw the "launch" of the SCM (supply chain management) industry, consisting of vendors, consultants, analysts, watch groups, specialized reports, and numerous internal efforts. The pace remains full speed ahead; see, for example, the supply chain operations reference (SCOR) model (www.supply-chain.org).

Much of the work in SCM from the mid 1990s until 2004 or 2005 focused on the creation of a centralized planning process and a centralized data view of the status of the organization's manufacturing and distribution activities. Less emphasis was placed on the third pillar of the SCM triangle – the decision model or the analytics – the enterprise wide detailed level CPE. Certainly, basic matching engines were produced and used, but most relied on heuristics despite the promise shown by linear programming (LP) in the Harris work (Leachman et al 1996) to handle the complexity of demand-supply networks in semiconductor manufacturing.

Why Use Optimization?

In macroeconomics and financial engineering, a well established concept is the "efficiency frontier" (also called production possibility frontier). In macroeconomics, if an economy is operating below its efficiency frontier, an increase in one product as well as in other goods can be obtained by increasing overall economic efficiency. If an economy is operating at its efficiency frontier, any increase in one product requires reducing the quantity of all other goods produced in the same period. Obviously in practice, there are multiple dimensions to this curve which can be education, transportation, or medicine. In finance, a similar pattern exists between risk and return: more risk, higher return; less risk, less return.

Supply Chain (demand-supply network) effectiveness & efficiency

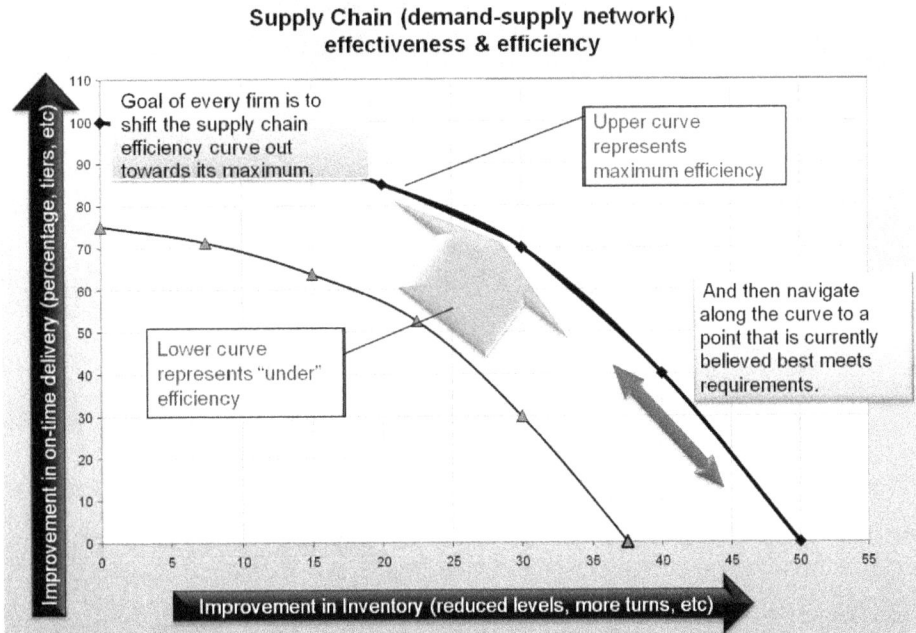

Goal of every firm is to shift the supply chain efficiency curve out towards its maximum.

Upper curve represents maximum efficiency

Lower curve represents "under" efficiency

And then navigate along the curve to a point that is currently believed best meets requirements.

Improvement in on-time delivery (percentage, tiers, etc)

Improvement in Inventory (reduced levels, more turns, etc)

A similar concept can be applied in supply chains. As in macroeconomics, the efficiency frontier has multiple dimensions, consisting of inventory, on-time delivery, customer satisfaction, profit, revenue, stability, growth of market, etc. For illustrative purposes we will have two dimensions (a) improvements in inventory performance (e.g., turns, excess, shelf life), and (b) improvements in on-time delivery or OTD (e.g., meeting request date, finding acceptable commit date, meeting commit date).

Just as in macroeconomics, if a supply chain is at its efficiency frontier, improving inventory requires reducing OTD. As Shobrys and Frazier (2003) make clear, few supply chains are operating at their efficiency frontier.

Therefore, the goal of each firm is to first shift the curve outward towards the efficiency frontier; then, the firm will navigate along the curve with great precision to the point that it believes best meets current market requirements.

A smarter mathematical model (planning engine) can directly improve a firm's performance. Let's look at the following simple example

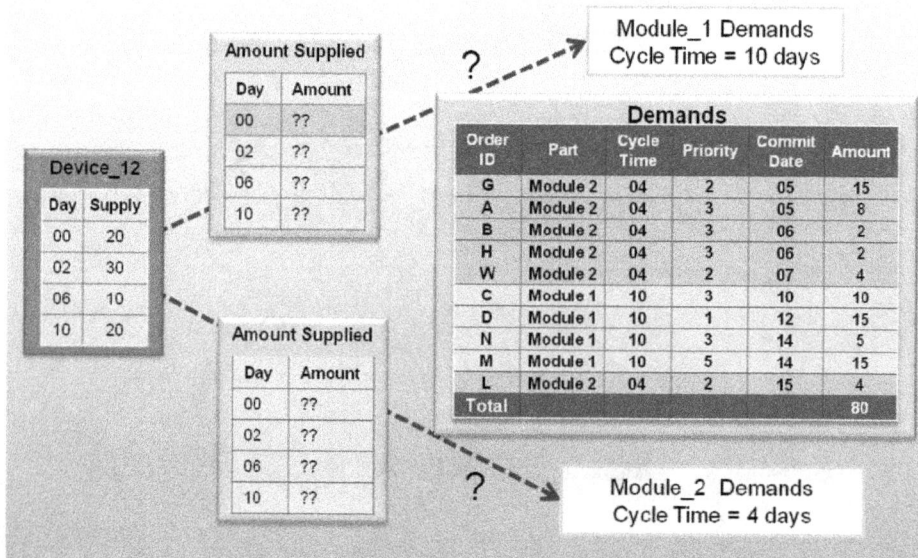

Assume a firm makes two products: Module_1 and Module_2, and both modules require Device_12 as their only component part. The time it takes to produce Module_1 and Module_2 is 10 and 4 days, respectively.

Once a unit of Device_12 is allocated to either Module_1 or Module_2, work begins immediately to make the module. If 3 units of Device_12 are allocated to Module_1 on day 2, then 3 units of Module_1 are available to meet demand on day 12 (=2+10). Similarly, if 4 units of Device_12 are allocated to Module_2 on day 6, then 4 units of Module_2 are available to meet demand on day 10 (=4+6).

The anticipated supply of Device_12 and the demand is shown in the diagram. The primary task of the central planning engine in this simple scenario is to allocate the anticipated supply of Device_12 to produce Module_1 and Module_2 so as to best meet demand and minimize inventory.

The algorithm for scoring "On-time Delivery (OTD" is: (a) if the demand is met on time or early the OTD score is 0; (b) if the demand is late the smaller of the number of days late and -5 is divided by the demand priority. The OTD scoring mechanism is designed only to be illustrative.

Below, two different search mechanisms come up with different allocations.

	Demands				Method 1			
ID	Part	Priority	Commit Date	Amt	Alloc Date	Stock Date	Delta	OTD Score
D	Module 1	1	12	15	00	10	02	00
G	Module 2	2	05	15	02	06	-01	-0.5
W	Module 2	2	07	4	00	04	03	00
L	Module 2	2	15	4	02	06	09	00
A	Module 2	3	05	8	02	06	-01	-0.33
B	Module 2	3	06	2	02	06	00	00
H	Module 2	3	06	2	06	10	-04	-1.33
C	Module 1	3	10	10	06	16	-06	-1.67
N	Module 1	3	14	5	10	20	-06	-1.67
M	Module 1	5	14	15	10	20	-06	-1.0
					On Time Delivery Score			-6.50
					Inventory Days			78

Demands					Method 2			
ID	Part	Priority	Commit Date	Amt	Alloc Date	Stock Date	Delta	OTD Score
D	Module 1	1	12	15	02	12	00	00
G	Module 2	2	05	15	00	04	01	00
W	Module 2	2	07	4	02	06	01	00
L	Module 2	2	15	4	06	10	05	00
A	Module 2	3	05	8	02	06	-01	-0.33
B	Module 2	3	06	2	02	06	00	00
H	Module 2	3	06	2	02	06	00	00
C	Module 1	3	10	10	06	16	-06	-1.67
N	Module 1	3	14	5	10	20	-06	-1.67
M	Module 1	5	14	15	10	20	-06	-1.0
					On Time Delivery Score			-4.67
					Inventory Days			39

The first set of columns under "Demands" repeat the demand information. It is the order identifier, the type of part, the priority of the demand, the commit date to meet this demand and the amount of the demand.

The second set of columns under "Method 1" is the allocation of supply of device_12 to produce either Module_1 or Module_2 to meet demand. The row for demand D for Module_1 can be read as follows: 15 units from the supply of Device_12 available on day 00 are allocated to meet this demand. Fifteen units of Module_1 comes to stock (is completed) on day 10 and is allocated to demand D. Since the commit date for demand D is day 12 and the supply is available on day 10, the supply is 2 days earlier (this is the delta column). The OTD (on time delivery) score is 0.

Observe that method 2 improves both on-time delivery (-4.67 compared to -6.50) and inventory (39 compared to 78) in comparison to method 1, moving the firm closer its efficiency frontier. **The "smarter" planning engine makes a direct impact on the firm's performance**.

The table below illustrates a third allocation where on-time delivery is improved (-4.33 compared to -4.67) but inventory is increased (43 compared to 39). This is an example of moving along the curve of efficiency frontier. The smart engine is able to follow the firm's business rules and position the firm at the point on the efficiency frontier where it currently believes is optimal.

	Demands				Method 3			
ID	Part	Priority	Commit Date	Amt	Alloc Date	Stock Date	Delta	OTD Score
D	Module 1	1	12	15	02	12	00	00
G	Module 2	2	05	15	00	04	01	00
W	Module 2	2	07	4	02	06	01	00
L	Module 2	2	15	4	10	14	01	00
A	Module 2	3	05	8	02	06	-01	-0.33
B	Module 2	3	06	2	02	06	00	00
H	Module 2	3	06	2	06	10	-04	-1.33
C	Module 1	3	10	10	10	20	-10	-1.67
N	Module 1	3	14	5	00	10	04	00
M	Module 1	5	14	15	10	20	-06	-1.0
					On Time Delivery Score			-4.33
					Inventory Days			43

Best-Can-Do Enterprise Wide Central Planning Engines

Overview

The best-can-do (BCD) enterprise wide detailed central planning engine (CPE) is the control point for the flow of material or product within an organization, and focuses on how to best meet prioritized demand without violating temporal, asset (WIP and inventory), or capacity constraints. A CPE application minimizes prioritized demand tardiness and some aspects of cost, establishing a projected supply and synchronized targets for each element of the supply chain.

The core of the CPE process is matching assets with demand, which refers to aligning assets with demand in an intelligent manner to best meet demands. The alignment or match occurs across multiple facilities within the boundaries established by the manufacturing specifications, process flows, and business policies.

Assets include, but are not limited to, starts (manufacturing releases), work in progress (WIP), inventory, purchases, and capacity (manufacturing equipment and manpower). Demands include, but are not limited to, firm orders, forecasted orders, and inventory buffer. The matching must take into account manufacturing/production specifications and business guidelines. Manufacturing specifications and process flows include, but are not limited to, build options, bill of material (BOM), yields, cycle times, anticipated date on which a unit of WIP will complete a certain stage of manufacturing (called a receipt date), capacity consumed, substitutability of one part for another (substitution), the determination of the actual part type after testing (called binning or sorting), and shipping times. Business guidelines include, but are not limited to, frozen zones (no change can be made on supplies requested), demand priorities, priority tradeoffs, preferred suppliers, and inventory policy. Many of the manufacturing specification and business guideline values will often change during the planning horizon (time effective).

The creation of a CPE plan requires a solver (sometimes referred to as a model or an engine) with the following core features:

1. Method(s) to represent the (potential) material flows in production, business policies, constraints, demand priorities, current locations of asset, etc., and relate all this information to exit demand;
2. The ability to capture asset quantities and manufacturing specifications (parameters);
3. Search mechanism(s) to generate a balanced supply chain plan, relate the outcome to demand, and modify the plan to improve the match;
4. A means to display and explain the results of the best-can-do match.

The first task of any "best-can-do" CPE is to "flow material" and maintain a "feasible material flow." Simply put, the CPE must decide a sequence of manufacturing starts to produce finished goods, and for each start the CPE places into the plan, the required component parts and capacity must be available and the manufacturing activity must be permitted on that day (e.g., it is not a shutdown day). For example, in the flow shown below, if the CPE decides to manufacture 10 cards on day 10 to be completed on day 14 to meet a customer's demand, then on day 10 it must have 20 modules and tool/equipment capacity for the manufacturing process to consume. Typically, the CPE handles this requirement either implicitly with material balance equations or explicitly with explosion and implosion.

Explosion and implosion are the core processes of the CPE which either move work units (WIP or starts) forward (implosion) to project completed parts or backward (explosion) to determine starts required across the bill-of-material (BOM) supply chain following the appropriate manufacturing data such as cycle time, yield, capacity, and product structure. We typically use implosion to estimate what finished goods will be available to meet demand and explosion to estimate what starts are needed at what due dates to ensure meeting the existing demand on time.

Conserving Material Flow

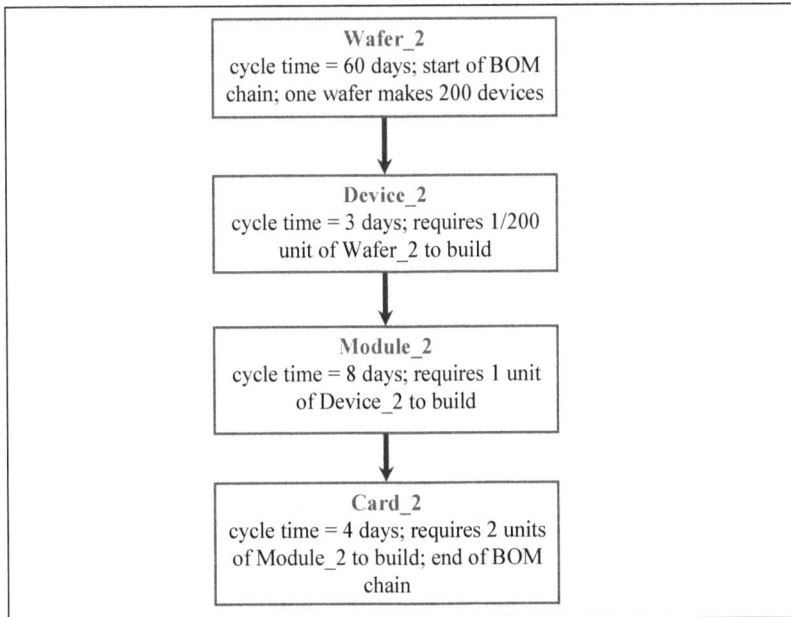

In the flow shown, the first manufacturing activity is the production of Wafer_ 2. This manufacturing activity has a cycle time of 60 days, i.e., it takes on average 60 days to take a raw wafer and create a completed wafer with the part ID Wafer_2. The second activity is device production. Creating one unit of Device_2 requires 3 days and consumes 1/200th unit of Wafer_2. Module_2 consumes one unit of Device_2 and takes 8 days to produce. Finally, Card_2 consumes two units of Module_2 and takes 4 days to produce.

Implosion can be illustrated with the following example. Manufacturing estimates that four units of Device_2 will be available or completed on day 10. This is called a projected receipt. If manufacturing immediately uses these four units to produce Module_2, on day 18 (10 + "Module_2 cycle time" = 10+8 = 18) four units of Module_2 will be completed. Continuing the projection process, the four units of Module_2 are immediately used to create two units of Card_2, which will be available on day 22 (18 + "Card_2 cycle time" = 18+4 = 22). The implosion process enables manufacturing to estimate the future supply of finished goods.

Explosion can be illustrated with an example. To meet demand for one unit of Card_2 on day 20, the plant must have two (completed) units of Module_2 available on day 16 (20 – "Card_2 cycle time" = 20 – 4 = 16). This generates an exploded demand of two units of Module_2 with a due date of day 16. To continue the explosion process, to produce the two units of Module_2, the plant must have two units of Device_2 available on day 8 (16 – "Module_2 cycle time" = 16 – 8 = 8). Next, the device demand is exploded creating a demand for 2/200th units of Wafer_2 on day 5 (= 8 – 3). This exploded information creates the guidelines for manufacturing to meet existing demand. For example, the device department must start production of two units of Device_2 no later than day 5 to meet the demand for one unit of Card_2 on day 20. Since the cycle time to produce Wafer_2 is 60 days, it needs to have one already in production and close to completion.

Within the explosion and implosion process is a method called "demand pegging." This method links each allocation of an asset or creation of a start with either a specific exit demand, or, at a minimum, the demand class or priority (relative importance of demand) associated with the exit demand being supported. Using the explosion example described above, if the exit demand for one unit of Card_2 on day 20 has a demand class of 3, each exploded demand will carry that demand class with it. Therefore, the units of Module_2 that are started on day 8 will have a demand class of 3. Similarly, if 3 units of Card_2 are desired on day 20 for a customer with demand class 5, then 6 units of Module_2 to be started on day 8 will also have a demand class of 5. The total required starts picture on day 8 is 8 (2+6), with 2 units with demand class 3 and 6 units with demand class 5. If by chance, there is only enough capacity on day 8 to start 2 units of Module_2, they will be allocated to the more important demand (demand class 3).

Challenges of Scope and Scale

"The great 20th century revelation that complex systems can be generated by the relationships among simple components" (Goldman 2004) applies to supply chain planning (and almost all aspects of planning, scheduling, and dispatch) (Little 1992).

Although simply creating a feasible central plan which maintains material balance, observes date effectivity, obeys business rules, captures existing WIP and inventory, and does a rough job at meeting demand is by itself challenging, it is no longer sufficient for a firm to remain competitive. The failure to "create a more accurate assessment of supply" forces the firm to compensate with slack or inefficiencies that leaves it at a competitive disadvantage.

Yet many companies continue to labor with rules of thumb assisted by multiple spreadsheets. Invariably, this leads to disconnected processes and inefficiencies. The use of spreadsheets is pervasive in planning because the tool is familiar and readily available.

While Excel can be a good place to start, we have found -- after working with several companies -- that there are some issues with Excel-based tools.

1. Spreadsheets don't often have the latest data because the data updates from corporate systems are not automated or systematized.

2. Sharing spreadsheets can be awkward. In an environment where the data is changing, often a number of copies of the same schedule can exist, each slightly different. Formats change and considerable manual effort is required to resynchronize the spreadsheets when spreadsheets are passed from one person to another

3. Planning and scheduling issues can sometimes be complex, and complicated spreadsheets may be needed to represent the material and capacity relationships. Many such spreadsheets simply collapse under their own weight.

4. Many of the business rules and heuristics rules embedded in the spreadsheets are lost when a planner leaves his or her job.

5. Excel lacks the required optimization, simulation and/or statistical tools needed to support rapid decision making. To get around this, complex rules of thumb are embedded in the worksheet which may not stay relevant as business conditions change.

Modern planning software addresses these deficiencies by using a central database that can store multiple scenarios and provide extensive "what-if" capability, while maintaining connectivity to desktop tools like Excel for reporting. A quick comparison of spreadsheets versus an enterprise planning tool is reproduced below.

	Spreadsheet	Enterprise Planning Tool
Able to optimize with respect to business drivers	Partially and informally	Yes. Business objectives can be modeled within an overall cost function.
Able to compare different alternatives	Only to the extent that the scenario comparison is programmed in the spreadsheet.	Not only is a scheduling tool able to compare scenarios, it is often able to identify and present the most promising scenarios to the scheduler.
Able to consider multiple constraints like capacity, resources, and raw material availability simultaneously	Ability to consider multiple constraints varies depending on the ability and talent of the scheduler.	Yes. For each decision the impact on the entire schedule is considered to evaluate the quality of the decision.
Ability to cope with conflicting requirements	Usually only a subset of the conflicting requirements are considered	Yes.
Ability to consolidate data	Normally requires manual synchronization with systems of record.	Automatic synchronization using a database.
Quality of achievable plan	Acceptable	Usually the best possible based on identified cost criteria.

Reference List

Arntzen, B., Brown, G., Harrison, T., and Trafton, L. (1995), "Global Supply Chain Management at Digital Equipment Corporation," *Interfaces* 25(1), pp. 69 – 93.

Davenport, T. (2006), "Competing on Analytics," Harvard Business Review, January 2006, pp. 1 – 9.

Denton, B., Forrest, J., and Milne, R.J. (2006b), "Methods for Solving a Mixed Integer Program for Semiconductor Supply Chain Optimization at IBM," *Interfaces*, Vol. 36, No. 5, September – October 2006, pp. 386 – 399.

Duchessi, P. (1987), "The Conceptual Design for a Knowledge Based System as Applied to the Production Planning Process," *Expert Systems for Business*, B. Silverman (ed) pp. 163 – 194

Fogarty, D. and Hoffman, T. (1983), *Production and Inventory Management*, Cincinnati, Ohio, South-West Publishing.

Fox, M. (1983), "Constraint Directed Search: A Case Study of Job Shop Scheduling," Technical Report, CMU-R1-TR-83-22, Robotics Institute, Carnegie-Mellon University, Pittsburg, PA.

Galbraith, J. (1973), *Designing Complex Organizations*, Addison-Wesley.

Glover, F., Jones, G., Karney, D., Klingman, D., and Mote, J. (1979), "An Integrated Production, Distribution, and Inventory Planning System," *Interfaces*, Vol. 9, No. 5, pp. 21 – 35.

Goldman, S. (2004), "Science in the Twentieth Century," Great Courses on CD by the Teaching Company, Chantilly, VA.

Graves, R.J., Konopka, J.M., and Milne, R.J. (1995), "Literature Review of Material Flow Control Mechanisms," *Production Planning and Control*, Vol. 6, No. 5, 395 – 403.

Hackman, S.T. and Leachman, R.C. (1989), "A General Framework for Modeling Production," *Management Science*, Vol. 35, No. 4, pp. 478 – 495.

Lee, H.L., Padmanabhan, V., and Whang, S. (1997), "Information Distortion in a Supply Chain: The Bullwhip Effect," *Management Science*, Vol. 43, No. 4 (special issue on frontier research in manufacturing and logistics), pp. 546 – 558.

Kempf, K. (1994), "Intelligently Scheduling Wafer Fabrication," *Intelligent Scheduling*, Morgan Kaufman Publishers, pp. 517 – 544 (Chapter 18).

Kempf, K. (2004), "Control-Oriented Approaches to Supply Chain Management in Semiconductor Manufacturing," Proceedings of the 2004 American Control Conference, Boston, MA, pp. 4563 – 4576.

Leachman, R., Benson, R., Liu, C., and Raar, D. (1996), "IMPReSS: An Automated Production Planning and Delivery-Quotation System at Harris Corporation - Semiconductor Sector," *Interfaces*, Vol. 26, No. 1, pp. 6 – 37.

Lin, G., Ettl, M., Buckley, S., Yao, D., Naccarato, B., Allan, R., Kim, K., Koenig, L. (2000), "Extended Enterprise Supply Chain Management at IBM Personal Systems Group and Other Divisions," *Interfaces*, 30(1), pp. 7 – 25.

Lyon, P., Milne, R.J., Orzell, R., Rice, R. (2001), "Matching Assets with Demand in Supply-Chain Management at IBM Microelectronics," *Interfaces*, 31:1, pp. 108 – 124.

Norden, P. (1993), "Quantitative Techniques in Strategic Alignment," *IBM Systems Journal*, Vol. 32, No. 1, pp. 180 – 197.

Shobrys, D. (2003), "History of APS," Supply Chain Consultants (www.supplychain.com), 460 Fairmont Drive, Wilmington, DE 19808, U.S.A.

Shobrys, D. and Fraser, J. (2003), "Planning for the next generation [supply chain planning]", *Manufacturing Engineer,* Volume 82, Issue 6, p. 10-13

Singh, H. (2007), "Personal Communication with Ken Fordyce" Supply Chain Consultants (www.supplychain.com), 5460 Fairmont Drive, Wilmington, DE 19808, U.S.A.

Sullivan, G. (1994), "Logistics Management System (LMS): Integrating Decision Technologies for Dispatch Scheduling in Semiconductor Manufacturing," *Intelligent Scheduling*, Morgan Kaufman Publishers, pp. 473 – 516.

Tayur, S., Ganeshan, R., and Magazine, M. (1998), *Quantitative Models for Supply Chain Management*, Kluwer Academic Publishers, Boston, MA.

Uzsoy, R., Lee, C., and Martin-Vega, L.A. (1992), "A Review of Production Planning and Scheduling Modules in the Semiconductor Industry, Part 1: System Characteristics, Performance Evaluation, and Production Planning," *IIE Transactions*, Scheduling Logistics, 24(4), pp. 47 – 60.

Uzsoy, R., Lee, C., and Martin-Vega, L.A. (1994), "A Review of Production Planning and Scheduling Modules in the Semiconductor Industry, Part 2: Shop Floor Control", *IIE Transactions*, Scheduling Logistics, 26(5), pp. 44 – 55.

Wang, C., Fordyce, K., Milne, R.J., and Orzell, R.A. (2008), "The IBM Advanced Planning System for Managing Next Generation Demand-Supply Networks," *International Journal of Integrated Supply Management*, Vol. 4, No. 1, pp. 125 – 140.

Woolsey, G. (1979), "Ten Ways to Go Down with Your MRP," *Interfaces*, Vol. 9, No. 5, pp. 77 – 80.

Modeling Issues for Food Manufacturers

By Quinn Freeman

Food manufacturers have been slow to adopt supply chain planning because their business environment does not fit the mold of traditional manufacturing, and the software that is normally available commercially is not geared to address their particular needs. However, some companies like Sunsweet Growers have taken advantage of configurable software to institutionalize supply chain planning practices that have paid hefty dividends.

One of the key measures for a cooperative like Sunsweet is the amount of money they can pay the growers for each ton of fruit. In recent years they have increased this by more than 30% - with much of this due to tighter planning and optimized scheduling. Better planning has resulted in increased asset utilization, lower transport costs, and a better match of inventory to demand.

This paper will examine some of the particular issues faced by food manufacturers, and how the supply chain planning process can be modified to accommodate these.

Specific Industry Challenges

Inverted Bills of Material

In food manufacturing, there are usually a few limited raw materials that get converted to multiple finished products. This has implications for both how the core functions of supply chain planning are executed and the software that is applicable.

Take for example the production of beef. The final products that are purchased consume some portion of the cow. It is not very useful to forecast the demand for final products independently if the only way to meet this demand would be to buy cattle with two heads and one tail. In other words, the demand forecast must be reconciled so that the mix of product demands is feasible in terms of the raw material.

The same issue occurs in the production of chicken. For the short term, the proportion of dark meat versus white meat that is available is fixed. A forecast that tries to predict the demand for white meat and dark meat independently is of little practical use. Certainly, excess production can be frozen, but this again erodes margins.

While all process manufacturers (paper products, refineries, etc.) have to reconcile the demand mix with the raw material supply, it is particularly important in food because of shelf life issues and consequently the inability to keep product in inventory over a long period.

Another issue with the bill of materials is that the mix of final products is controlled by how the raw material is processed, e.g., the ratio of ground meat versus steak or the ratio of ground meat with 80% fat content and ground meat with 90% fat content. The mix of final products is intimately tied to the production decisions.

Each mix also has its own revenue profile. The margin associated with a mix is constantly changing because of market considerations. The optimal mix from a margin point of view has to be constantly adapted to what will sell at the final product level, and what can be feasibly supplied.

Product Substitution

The food industry has many characteristics similar to consumer products. Chief among them is that consumers can and do substitute one product for another routinely. The substitution occurs within a product family (one cut of beef versus another) and also between families (chicken for beef). The substitution can be controlled somewhat through promotions and sales, but these efforts also erode margins.

The degree of substitution is determined by factors that are usually beyond the control of an individual manufacturer. They are determined by the retail strategy, the economic climate, and the overall supply of a particular commodity. The challenge for the individual manufacturer is how to retain acceptable margins within an environment of constantly changing prices and product demand.

Many manufacturers respond to the uncertainty by trying to "forward sell." For example, a manufacturer may try to lock in demand by discounting the anticipated supply through targeted sales. It is not uncommon in some industries to have 80 to 90% of the anticipated supply committed to orders one week ahead. While this is desirable from a management point of view, it does erode margins because the certainty of future orders comes at a cost.

Regulations and "Nuclear Accidents"

Food manufacturers have more than their share of regulatory oversight. While these rules are required to safeguard health, they have an impact on the ability to change manufacturing strategy and capability quickly. In supply chain management, flexibility is almost always traded against buffers like inventory and capacity. The lack of flexibility translates into additional inventory and slack capacity.

The lack of flexibility can be challenging in an environment where one-time events can affect demand or supply dramatically. For example, the discovery of a case of "mad cow" disease or the discovery of contamination in a food source can devastate the demand and supply assumptions that a company is working with. This is equivalent to a "nuclear accident." Unfortunately, these disruptions are becoming almost routine because of increased oversight and manufacturers who succumb to shortcuts due to the pressure of eroding margins.

Consolidation at the Retail Level

As retailers consolidate, the power in the food supply chain is shifting from the suppliers to the retailers. For supply chain management, the immediate effect is that manufacturers have to cope with reduced margins. At the same time, the retailers are demanding that the products delivered to them require minimal or no processing.

For manufacturers this means that the number of products that they manage increases dramatically. For food manufacturers, the demand is no longer for beef carcasses, but for particular kinds of meat packaged and wrapped ready for the shelf. The only way that a manufacturer can cope with the reduced margins and the need for additional processing is by constantly optimizing the mix of products, with respect to the available supply, the anticipated demand, and the margins that the marketplace will support.

Supply Restrictions

Supply restrictions can take many forms. Supply for some manufacturers is seasonal. This means that planning has to cover at least a season, and manufacturing has to be compressed into a short time interval. Secondly, the supply cannot usually be varied within a growing cycle. This may be as short as 4 to 8 weeks for products like chicken to more than 12 months for products like beef. Third, some manufacturers operate with a fixed supply base. For example, certain food manufacturers are restricted to growers in a particular region, a particular cooperative, or a particular type of supply (e.g., "organic").

It is not that supply restrictions do not occur in other industries. It is just that in food manufacturing, supply restrictions are the norm rather than the exception.

An Improved Planning Process

The complexity of the food manufacturing process does not mean that supply chain planning is irrelevant. In fact, companies have shown that precisely because of this complexity, optimized planning can provide very significant benefits.

Many companies get discouraged in their search for supply chain planning software because the software is not adaptable to the food manufacturing environment, and vendors tend to push a methodology that cannot be practically implemented in the food supply chain. Traditional Sales and Operation Planning (S&OP) does not work well because its execution tends to be too slow and cannot accommodate the constantly changing environment.

Demand Planning

Planning Data Repository

Single Data Repository to facilitate
- Security and Data Management,
- User access and role based security
- ERP data interchange

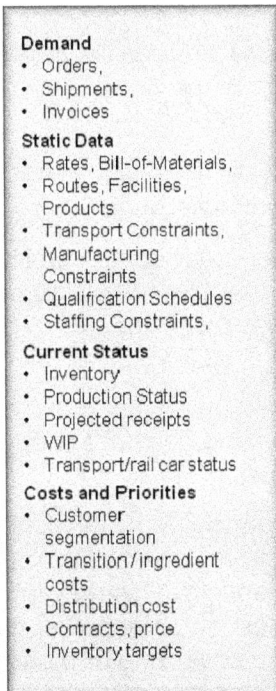

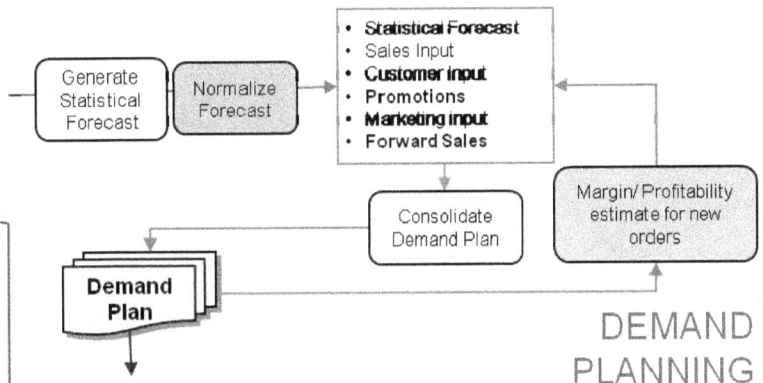

Demand
- Orders,
- Shipments,
- Invoices

Static Data
- Rates, Bill-of-Materials,
- Routes, Facilities, Products
- Transport Constraints,
- Manufacturing Constraints
- Qualification Schedules
- Staffing Constraints,

Current Status
- Inventory
- Production Status
- Projected receipts
- WIP
- Transport/rail car status

Costs and Priorities
- Customer segmentation
- Transition/ingredient costs
- Distribution cost
- Contracts, price
- Inventory targets

Generate Statistical Forecast

Normalize Forecast

- Statistical Forecast
- Sales Input
- Customer input
- Promotions
- Marketing input
- Forward Sales

Consolidate Demand Plan

Margin/Profitability estimate for new orders

Demand Plan

DEMAND PLANNING

The basic collaborative process for demand planning carries over from other industries with some modifications:

1. The collaborative input must also include promotions, as well as any forward sales because these can significantly influence the demand.

2. Any statistical forecast needs to be normalized so that it is feasible from a raw material point of view. The initial statistical forecast can be thought of as "what could sell." The normalized forecast is "what can be sold" given what can be produced using raw materials. Normally in other industries, this is done in the planning engine. However, the raw material constraints are so inflexible in food manufacturing that this is best carried out up front.

3. A separate and distinct process is needed to estimate if an order is profitable given the current demand plan and available supply. Again, this is normally done in the planning or scheduling processes for other industries. In fact, the evaluation is usually only to decide if a given order can be filled.

    In food manufacturing, because the margins are heavily dependent on the mix of products, this evaluation must be done early in the planning process, for two reasons:

    -   Supply in the short term is relatively fixed and new orders must take the short term availability into account.

    -   Pricing tends to be flexible and order dependent. A profitability analysis is needed to make sure that the correct prices are used to encourage the sale of excess products.

Supply Planning

While the basic step for supply/demand balancing does not change, there are a few key differences from other industries.

First, the short term supply and demand is normally fairly inflexible. The supply/demand balancing role is to provide the requirements for purchasing the raw materials and capacity planning. This may involve future contracts, price hedging, spot purchases, and manpower planning. For this reason, the planning horizon needs to cover one or more planning cycles.

The short-term demand plan used for order promising and margin analysis has to be extended using higher level business projections. The level of detail used for order promising is generally too detailed for projecting longer term demand. The business projections are normally done at the aggregated product level (for example "primal" in the case of beef).

Planning Data Repository

Single Data Repository to facilitate
- **Security and Data Management.**
- **User access and role based security**
- **ERP data interchange**

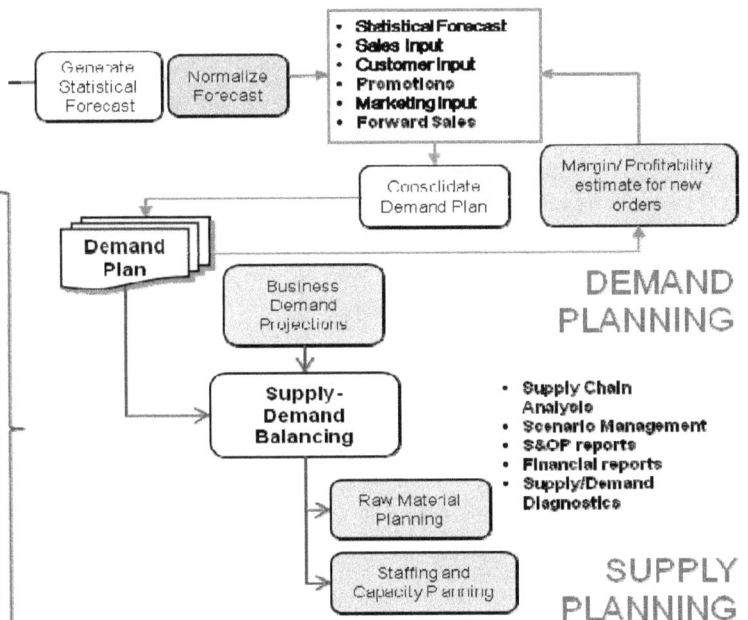

Demand
- Orders,
- Shipments,
- Invoices

Static Data
- Rates, Bill-of-Materials,
- Routes, Facilities, Products
- Transport Constraints,
- Manufacturing Constraints
- Qualification Schedules
- Staffing Constraints,

Current Status
- Inventory
- Production Status
- Projected receipts
- WIP
- Transport/rail car status

Costs and Priorities
- Customer segmentation
- Transition / ingredient costs
- Distribution cost
- Contracts, price
- Inventory targets

Generate Statistical Forecast → Normalize Forecast →
- Statistical Forecast
- Sales Input
- Customer Input
- Promotions
- Marketing Input
- Forward Sales

Consolidate Demand Plan

Margin/ Profitability estimate for new orders

Demand Plan

Business Demand Projections

DEMAND PLANNING

Supply-Demand Balancing

- Supply Chain Analysis
- Scenario Management
- S&OP reports
- Financial reports
- Supply/Demand Diagnostics

Raw Material Planning

Staffing and Capacity Planning

SUPPLY PLANNING

In some cases, the manpower planning and raw material planning can be included explicitly in a quantitative model that balances supply and demand. This is the preferred method because then the analysis can be based on maximizing margins.

Scheduling

Because of the need to constantly react to changes in demand and pricing, the short term demand plan is directly linked to the schedule. The main purpose of the scheduling process is to feasibly meet the orders within the supply restriction already in place by assigning specific production activities to shipments.

Planning Data Repository

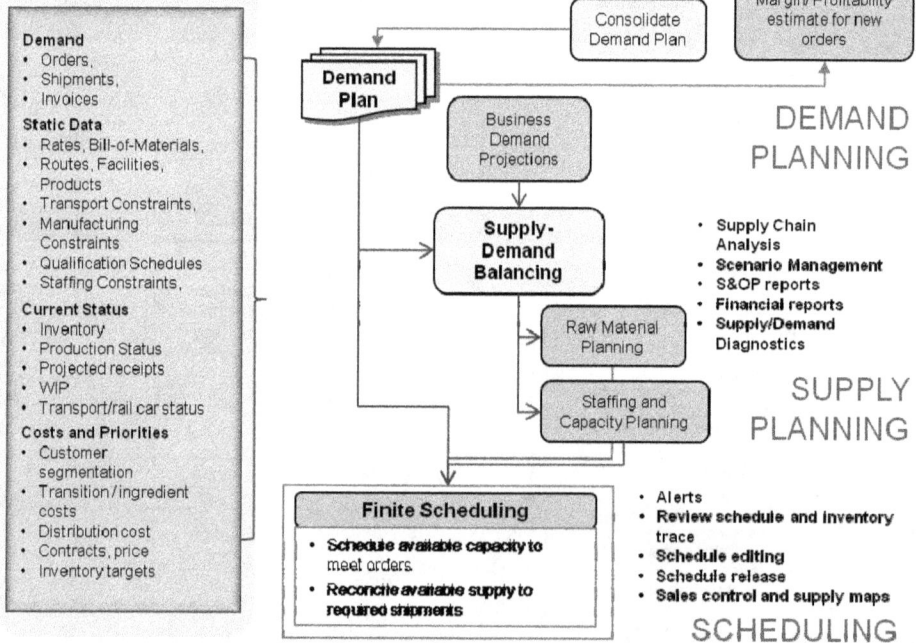

This is different from many other scheduling processes in the process industry where the scheduling works to build inventory of a product which is then consumed by orders. Indeed, benefits can be significantly increased if the scheduling process is linked directly to the shipment process.

Lessons from the Trenches

Supply chain planning in the process industry has had qualified success. All too often, vendors and consultants have tried to transfer technology and processes developed for the discrete industry directly to the process environment without fully understanding the special needs of the process industry.

In this chapter, we reproduce a series of interviews with industry leaders that have successfully introduced supply chain planning to process companies.

An Interview with ED HULLER

Edward Huller is President of Alden Consulting Group, which is focused on assisting companies with the development and implementation of supply chain strategies. He retired from Borden Chemical, Inc. in 2003 as Vice President, Global Supply Chain and Information Technology. Ed began his career in corporate logistics with Dow Chemical. Co. in 1970.

His responsibilities have included production planning, logistics, purchasing, international distribution, economic evaluation, order fulfillment and process design.

When Ed Huller was hired by Borden, Inc. in 1999, he was given the task of establishing a supply chain organization and instituting mechanisms for better forecasting, production planning, and inventory management.

What was it like in the chemicals division when you started?

Huller: The division was made up of more than 50 plants, each doing their own scheduling and inventory controls. There were no processes and no tools in place for forecasting or coordinating activities between and among the plants. Each plant set its own schedule based on open orders.

Where do you start with a situation like that?

Huller: We had to establish an understanding and a belief in the value of resource planning. We began by bringing in people who understood planning, who had experience in how to do planning. Only then could we introduce the tools. We had to establish the process first. Then we could search for tools and technologies to support the process.

Were you trying to establish a corporate planning function?

Huller: No. We wanted to deal with planning at a regional level. Each plant had its orders and its own capabilities, but there was no awareness or consideration of what other plants in the area could do or their limitations. With a regional plan, we could balance out the capabilities and demands and get more out of the collection of resources. We established new regional planners who developed what amounts to a rough-cut capacity plan for the region and then developed the schedules accordingly.

What do you consider your biggest success in this project?

Huller: I guess that would be at a forest products business unit in Seattle. A senior executive there said to me, "This is the kind of information I've always needed to run my business." For success in a project of this nature, you need individuals with the vision and the confidence to understand the areas that can be improved, and then take it on as their own.

What were your biggest challenges?

Huller: People's resistance to change - especially at the more remote sites. They were doing their own scheduling reasonably well and weren't interested in changing that. They did not understand the opportunities for improving overall performance across multiple sites because they had no awareness of what went on at those other sites and, in some cases, achieving overall performance might not result in the best performance at their own site.

What are the major risks and challenges in establishing a planning process?

Huller: It's all in the people issues and education. I guess the biggest risk would be in not staying the course long enough to achieve your objectives. This is not a quick fix - it takes time. The technology is the easy part. Getting people to change their behavior and thought processes when they've been operating successfully in a different mode - that's hard. You have to get the right mentality in place - then you can use the tools. The "black box" approach doesn't work. You make people use something they don't understand, and the first time there's a problem, they don't know how to interpret it or fix it.

What advice would you offer to someone about to embark on a project like this one?

Huller: Have a strong business case. Document the need for change, the cost of the project, and the expected results. A project like this can't be functionally led. Business leaders who understand the dollars and cents must lead it. It takes a strong commitment to engage people with knowledge and experience to make it happen as quickly as possible. We hired in good people who had lived through this before. They helped us sustain during the times when other companies would have faltered

An interview with JEFFREY HOWARD

Jeffrey Howard is an independent consultant with more than 20 years of experience in engineering and managing supply chain solutions and processes. He has spent many years working with refining companies to improve their crude and blend scheduling processes both as a consultant and as an employee at Marathon Oil.

Why is it difficult to implement an advanced scheduling solution in a refinery environment?

Howard: Most refineries are generally operated using a combination of tools ranging from planning using LP to rules of thumb. Experienced refinery schedulers and operators know what works and have developed informal rules that govern the way they perform certain tasks related to the supply chain. This is not a bad thing, since they can run the refinery reasonably well most of the time. These same rules, however, can get in the way of their considering and accepting new, sophisticated tools that could help them make the most of the resources they have available.

Are you saying that most refineries don't use computerized scheduling?

Howard: That's right, unless you consider Excel to be a computerized scheduler. Seriously, many refining companies have tried to develop schedulers or have attempted to implement commercial software scheduling solutions with disappointing results. So, most refineries are still run with those rules of thumb along with the experience of some very talented and overworked individuals.

Why have they been unsuccessful in their attempts to adopt better tools?

Howard: I think in many cases it's because they tried to bite off too big a task. A refinery operation is a very complex business. The schedulers must contend with very complex processing equipment. The output, volumes and qualities change based on the feed and operating conditions. This is a much more complex environment than is found in a typical manufacturing environment where operations and recipes are not changing constantly. Trying to manage all of these variables with an optimization system is very challenging because you can't afford mistakes that underutilize resources, disappoint customers, or miss demand swings.

What's the solution, then?

Howard: You have to focus on the ins and outs of the process — that's really where the largest rate of return is. Optimizing the scheduling and management of the refinery itself should wait until the ins and outs are under control. Think about a refinery where the raw material is coming in faster than it can be processed. You have a fleet of tankers lined up waiting their turn to unload, and each one of those tankers is costing you money while it's just sitting there. Good scheduling on the input side can really pay off in reduced demurrage fees and supplying the best crude mix to the crude unit(s). The buyers buy crude from a large number of sources with a wide range of quality and specific characteristics. The traders are looking for the best deal on a daily basis. Because the refinery has a somewhat limited ability to pick and choose, they must carefully track those different lots through the tanks, mixing and isolating to get the right material into the process for the specific products. Properly matching the mix to the demand is a high value activity.

It sounds like optimization could be of great value.

Howard: Absolutely, but it's hard to go into a company and just install optimization. The word "optimization" makes people's eyes roll. There is little belief in the "magic red button" that will solve all of their problems. I like to start with what they do now and introduce a possible solution that can help them build on what they have. I take their manual schedule and put that into the system and let the simulation show the result. They can see problems before they occur. Let's say the manual schedule looks good when looking at the whole day at once, but the simulator might show several hours in the middle of the shift where a component goes negative. That kind of shortage in real life is a major problem. When a software solution shows a shortage before the day starts, and adjustments can be made to avoid the problem, then there is real value. That kind of demonstration sends a very powerful message. A software product that can show that kind of value is generally very well received and drives acceptance of new tools.

An Interview with JANE LEE

Jane Lee set up and ran an S&OP process for a billion dollar DuPont business for more than 10 years. During this time, she introduced key improvements in technology and processes that lowered inventories, increased order fulfillment and lowered supply chain costs. After retiring from DuPont, Jane has worked as a consultant helping numerous companies improve their tactical planning.

Why do you think that supply chain management has not had more success?

Lee: Many companies continue to try to improve the supply chain through a massive soup-to-nuts "supply chain improvement project." Such projects frequently share common attributes:

- Led by consultants who have never actually worked in the supply chain

- Driven by a single software configuration or supply chain management theory

- Require re-engineering business processes to fit the software or theory

- Offer a pre-determined, "one size fits all" solution

- Require changing almost all supply chain functions, processes, procedures simultaneously

- Promise a one-time "magic bullet" to solve all supply chain issues

Dramatic and sustainable results come not from formal projects but through talented professionals with years of experience solving real life problems as they arise and institutionalizing the means to prevent recurrence. Evolution, rather than revolution, works best. What works is a pragmatic approach which concentrates on re-engineering the supply chain continually and to fit the business needs, rather than reengineering once to fit a particular theory or software package.

In your opinion, what is the single biggest mistake that companies make in trying to improve planning?

Lee: Companies don't pay enough attention to data. Successful supply chain management is highly data intensive. It cannot be done without widespread access to data, appropriate and flexible systems, and people who know both the business and the systems well enough to turn data into information.

Companies also must respect the limits of their data. The strength of a six-month detailed planning horizon is that it rests on real, mix-adjusted and capacity-feasible schedules and reliable, SKU-level forecasts. There is very little point in defining complex methods to optimize if the available data will not support it.

Many companies try to set up the processes without looking to see if the data will support them. As a result, when they try to implement the processes, they inevitably fail.

Besides data, are there other things that you need to pay attention to?

Lee: Yes, the organization has to be committed to improving the supply chain over a long period. A completed process is a dead process. If the business is alive and growing, the processes and systems had better be, too. Lasting change is incremental change. And the right incremental changes at the right times can make step-change improvements in business results.

Each incremental change must work toward optimizing the whole, not the parts. Neither maximizing customer service nor optimizing manufacturing yield nor minimizing working capital nor meeting regional targets is the goal. The goal is to be a profitable global business over the long term, and that requires finding the best balance for the bottom line.

Secondly, you need to respect the expertise which already exists in the organization. The best knowledge of what needs to be improved – and of how it can be done – is likely to come from those already doing the work. Success in implementing change is directly proportional to buy-in from key executors of the process. Buy-in is directly proportional to involvement in design of the change. Management support is critical but not sufficient; the "troops" will make the difference.

An Interview with ED MAHLER

Ed Mahler has over 30 years experience in implementing, supporting and running supply chain systems. At DuPont his assignments included stints in manufacturing, IT, and Corporate Plans. An early proponent of exploiting emerging IT technology, he established a task force at DuPont to implement and utilize expert systems technology. For the last 10 years, Ed has been recognized as a thought leader in supply chain management and has advised numerous corporate clients on how to set up and manage world-class supply chains.

You've said that the four dimensions of value provide a framework that companies can use to build understanding and improve IT choices.

Mahler: Yes, absolutely. I think it's very important for the various constituencies within a company to understand that there is a natural tension among them. As an example, business unit leaders need Functionality and Adaptability to be able to respond to their marketplaces, while corporate staff management places a high importance on Integration and Leverage to reduce costs and insure reliability.

Surely, both have legitimate claims.

Mahler: Yes, and that's the point. Internal bickering is counterproductive and all would be better off if that energy would be used to find the correct balance. The four factors account for 100% of the value, but you can't get all of the value from just one or two factors – there must be a mix of the four. Frequently, well-intentioned persons with differing beliefs of the value mix cannot have a constructive dialog. The exact emphasis on each of these dimensions will be different for each company and businesses within the company – and may, in fact, change over time as business conditions and objectives change.

So the "four dimensions" is a framework for discussion?

Mahler: Actually, it's a tool to enable understanding, facilitate constructive dialog, and guide strategic IT sourcing decisions. I believe people inherently understand that there are tradeoffs to be made and have a preconception (different due to their own experience and current assignment) of which dimensions to favor. This framework allows objective consensus building and organizational alignment for an IT sourcing strategy, be it "best of breed" for some functions and highly leveraged for others.

How do you make the tradeoffs, then?

Mahler: That's the essence of organizational alignment. There's no universal "right" answer, and no answer will be all one way or the other. There's always a combination of factors that will be most advantageous overall for the health of the organization. It's finding the right mix – the right tradeoff among these four factors – that spells success. If a company is in a stable market, with stable products (long lifecycles) and processes, efficiency will be of utmost importance, and the mix will favor Leverage at the expense of Adaptability. Functionality and Integration are always important, but in this case less so than Leverage. Another company in fast moving markets with short product cycles will be driven more toward Adaptability and Functionality and less toward Leverage. The four dimensions framework helps companies see these relationships and hopefully better understand what's good for the company as a whole.

Has this viewpoint helped companies arrive at better position vis-à-vis technology decisions?

Mahler: Oh, yes. And it's interesting to see how viewpoints can change. A business user, for example, might be the company's strongest advocate for Adaptability, then move into a corporate management position and suddenly switch sides and start pushing for more Integration and Leverage. The model explains the change in perspective.

An Interview with DON SHOBRYS

Don has extensive experience in implementing supply chain planning tools in over 70 Fortune 1000 companies, including BP, Champion International, Cypress Semiconductor, DuPont, Exxon Chemicals, Goodyear, IBM, Kraft, Monsanto, Philip Morris, and Upjohn. The former COO of Chesapeake Decision Sciences, Don has helped global organizations manage the change issues, developed strategies for minimizing risk of improvement projects, and worked to develop and offer sustainable solutions that return long-term value for organizations worldwide.

What do you see as a big challenge today for supply chain improvement?

Shobrys: Very few companies are starting large-scale technology projects today – corporate-wide ERP or supply chain systems – and as a result, technology spending is limited to smaller, more directed projects. The problem is that many of these initiatives are driven from the perspective of minimizing IT costs and that can run counter to the objective of providing opportunities for local innovation and local experimentation. There are a lot of drivers for that kind of local activity. Look across the business and you'll see all kinds of variation – commodity vs. specialized products, bulk vs. packaged goods, batch vs. continuous production. And businesses aren't static. They change over time and adaptation is required. Standardization efforts work against these needs. Companies are in an uncertain state as to how much local experimentation or adaptation they should allow. This results in contention between the business and the IT organizations. Over the last 5 or 10 years, much emphasis has been placed on defining and adhering to the corporate standard. It also seems that one of the things that has happened over the last 3 or 4 years is that businesses have been coming up with ways of getting around that.

Is that a good thing or a bad thing?

Shobrys: That depends – the business is interested in profit maximization. The primary focus of the technology gatekeepers is the minimization of IT costs. There are still a lot of opportunities to make relatively small IT investments that can provide significant benefits. If the focus is strictly on minimizing costs, a lot of these opportunities will be not considered. Unfortunately, when choosing a technology set, people tend to think about tools that will allow innovation at a local level. I think that's one of the most powerful things Microsoft has going for it – if you pick the Microsoft technology set there's a lot you can do at the local level and as a result that's where a great deal of informal development takes place – in Access and Excel, even to this day. The only drawback to this is that these activities are not recognized by the IT organization and may not be looked after from a long-term perspective.

So cost minimization shouldn't be allowed to override the needs of the business?

Shobrys: Right – there's little sensitivity to the fact that the different parts of the business are going to have to adapt to different operating characteristics and changing business conditions.

Specifically, what's the status of supply chain applications?

Shobrys: Supply chain applications are somewhat adrift. Since companies are no longer making long-term expenditures, projects are now defined on more of an incremental basis. But it doesn't seem like companies have well-established drivers for moving things forward on an incremental basis.

Are you saying there's a lack of strategic vision?

Shobrys: To some degree. It's almost as if when companies decided that they were no longer going to make those kinds of large scale expenditures, the supply chain dropped off the radar screen of key management initiatives. The need is still there – the world is not standing still, business environments continue to change – but it seems that the charter and the drive to move forward with business improvement has been lost in many companies.

What's the solution?

Shobrys: The solution is getting back to a focus on execution and looking for a mechanism to support a continuous improvement process in the business. The supply chain is still a fertile area for extracting more value out of the business. The incentive is there for management, but since they have decided not to go with the big-ticket projects, the drivers and owners have been lost in the organization. Ten or 15 years ago, a lot of supply chain initiatives were triggered locally. There's benefit from those (local) initiatives and you pick up additional synergies if there is some degree of coordination around them. If companies want to kick-start a genuine culture of supply chain improvement, they need to do two things: First, it's necessary to encourage ownership and motivation for improvement. Next, target business improvements and allow people to be "locally innovative" in pursuing them.

www.ingramcontent.com/pod-product-compliance
Lightning Source LLC
Chambersburg PA
CBHW051226200326
41519CB00025B/7269